Snort 3 QuickStart Pro

Detect malicious network activity, scan packets, generate alerts, and debug traffic for active intrusion prevention system (IPS)

Darvin Quolmar

Published by: GitforGits

Publisher: Sonal Dhandre

www.gitforgits.com

support@gitforgits.com

Printed in India

First Printing: July 2024

ISBN: 978-81-974165-3-8

Cover Design by: Kitten Publishing

Prologue

Working in cybersecurity, I've seen the ever-changing nature of the threats that affect our networks on a daily basis. Throughout my career, I've witnessed how the right tools can make a significant difference in protecting an organization's assets and data. Of all the useful tools out there, Snort has always been my favorite. Snort's robust features and flexibility have made it a cornerstone of many security operations, allowing us to detect and respond to threats quickly and efficiently.

When I first started working with Snort, I was drawn to its open-source nature and the thriving community that surrounds it. I liked how it wasn't just a static tool, but a platform that could be customized and extended to meet the specific needs of any organization. As I explored and implemented Snort in various environments over the years, I realized there was a need for a guide that could assist others in quickly understanding and leveraging Snort's true potential. That realization inspired me to create Snort 3 QuickStart Pro. I wanted to create something that would give cybersecurity, networking, and IT professionals a quick, practical guide to using Snort 3. This book will teach you how to successfully deploy, configure, and manage Snort in your network environment. Throughout this book, I emphasize real-world applications and useful insights. You'll learn how to configure Snort to monitor your network traffic, create and implement custom rules for detecting specific threats, and use preprocessors to improve detection capabilities. I also go over performance tuning and optimization, demonstrating how to scale Snort to handle high volumes of traffic without sacrificing detection accuracy.

One of Snort's distinguishing features is its ability to integrate with other tools and systems. I look at these integrations and show how you can use Snort in conjunction with other security solutions to create a comprehensive defense strategy. Whether you work for a small business or manage a large enterprise network, these integrations can significantly improve your security posture. Troubleshooting is another important aspect of using Snort effectively. In this book, I've included detailed sections on diagnosing and resolving common issues, so you can keep Snort running smoothly and reliably. You will learn how to analyze logs, debug rules, and fine-tune configurations for optimal results. The information in this book is specifically designed to help you become a proficient user of Snort. My goal is to provide you with the tools and knowledge you need to protect your network from the ever-increasing number of cybersecurity threats. With the techniques and strategies outlined in these pages, you will be better equipped to deploy Snort in your environment, manage its operations, and tailor it to your specific security requirements.

Thank you for choosing this book; I am confident that it will be a useful guide in your efforts to protect your digital assets.

Content

Preface

To help cybersecurity, networking, and information technology professionals learn Snort 3 fast, we've created the Snort 3 QuickStart Pro. This book offers practical insights into deploying and managing Snort in a variety of network environments, enabling you to effectively use Snort's powerful intrusion detection and prevention features.

The book begins with an introduction to Snort's architecture and configuration, then walks you through setting up Snort for various network scenarios. You will discover how to enhance detection capabilities by writing and implementing Snort rules, using preprocessors, and integrating dynamic modules. You will apply Snort to real-world network problems with the help of examples and detailed instructions. It further teaches performance tuning and optimization strategies, allowing you to handle high traffic loads while maximizing resource efficiency. The book later explains how to set up high availability settings, including redundancy and failover mechanisms, to ensure continuous protection.

In addition, a strong emphasis is placed on troubleshooting, with sections dedicated to diagnosing and resolving common issues encountered during Snort deployment and operation. You will learn to analyze logs, debug rules, and optimize configurations for maximum performance and accuracy. Upon completion, you will be able to deploy Snort 3, manage its operations, and adapt it to changing security needs. Equipped with clear explanations and hands-on exercises, this book enables you to improve your network security skills and respond effectively to cyber threats.

In this book you get skilled with:

- Up and running with setting up Snort 3 for a wide range of network types and security requirements.
- Write effective Snort rules to safeguard your network and identify threats with pinpoint accuracy.
- Maximize Snort's detection capabilities by utilizing preprocessors and dynamic modules.
- Improve performance and deal with heavy traffic loads by learning Snort's architecture.
- Setup failover and high availability measures.
- Check and fix frequent issues to keep Snort running smoothly and reliably.
- Use Snort's alerting and logging capabilities to oversee and manage network infrastructure.
- Combine Snort with additional tools for an integrated approach to network security administration.

GitforGits

Prerequisites

This book is for cybersecurity enthusiasts, networking professionals, information security analysts, security specialists and network security professionals to utilize Snort for deploying powerful IDS and IPS system in their business infrastructure. Knowing basics of networking and security concepts are sufficicent to begin with the book.

Codes Usage

Are you in need of some helpful code examples to assist you in your programming and documentation? Look no further! Our book offers a wealth of supplemental material, including code examples and exercises.

Not only is this book here to aid you in getting your job done, but you have our permission to use the example code in your programs and documentation. However, please note that if you are reproducing a significant portion of the code, we do require you to contact us for permission.

But don't worry, using several chunks of code from this book in your program or answering a question by citing our book and quoting example code does not require permission. But if you do choose to give credit, an attribution typically includes the title, author, publisher, and ISBN. For example, "Snort 3 QuickStart Pro by Darvin Quolmar".

If you are unsure whether your intended use of the code examples falls under fair use or the permissions outlined above, please do not hesitate to reach out to us at support@gitforgits.com.

We are happy to assist and clarify any concerns.

Acknowledgement

I owe a tremendous debt of gratitude to GitforGits, for their unflagging enthusiasm and wise counsel throughout the entire process of writing this book. Their knowledge and careful editing helped make sure the piece was useful for people of all reading levels and comprehension skills. In addition, I'd like to thank everyone involved in the publishing process for their efforts in making this book a reality. Their efforts, from copyediting to advertising, made the project what it is today.

Finally, I'd like to express my gratitude to everyone who has shown me unconditional love and encouragement throughout my life. Their support was crucial to the completion of this book. I appreciate your help with this endeavour and your continued interest in my career.

CHAPTER 1: GETTING STARTED WITH IDPS

Chapter Overview

Intrusion Detection Systems (IDS) and Intrusion Prevention Systems (IPS) are the cornerstones of network security, and we commence our exploration of these concepts in this chapter. When it comes to protecting digital assets, these systems are vital for spotting and reducing risks. We will look at how IDS and IPS work, how they differ, and why they're essential components of any comprehensive cybersecurity strategy. Next, we will take a look at Snort 3 and how it has evolved from previous versions and explores the key features and enhancements that make it an excellent choice for cybersecurity professionals. This section will introduce you to Snort's architecture, laying the groundwork for more advanced topics covered later in the book.

We will then move on to configuring a Linux environment for cybersecurity operations. This includes selecting the appropriate Linux distribution, installing necessary tools, and configuring your system to create a stable and secure Snort platform. In addition, we will walk you through the process of creating a virtual lab environment so that you can test and experiment with Snort in a controlled environment. These fundamental skills are essential for developing a resilient security infrastructure.

The chapter concludes by discussing the vital subject of network security and the ethical considerations that must be included. This section will go over best practices for ethical hacking and the importance of following legal guidelines when conducting security assessments. When you finish this chapter, you will have a solid grasp of the basics that will allow you to confidently jump into Snort 3 and the world of network security operations.

Understanding IDS and IPS

IDS and IPS are integral components of a comprehensive cybersecurity strategy, designed to protect networks from unauthorized access and malicious activities. As a cybersecurity professional, understanding the nuances of these systems is crucial for safeguarding digital assets. Both IDS and IPS monitor network traffic to detect and respond to threats, but they do so in distinct ways, each offering unique advantages. Their roles in modern cybersecurity frameworks have become more critical as organizations face an ever-evolving landscape of cyber threats.

What is an IDS?

An IDS is a tool that monitors network or system activities for malicious activities or policy violations. The primary function of an IDS is to detect unauthorized access and anomalous behavior, providing alerts to administrators when potential threats are identified.

IDS can be categorized into two main types: network-based intrusion detection systems (NIDS) and host-based intrusion detection systems (HIDS).

Network-Based Intrusion Detection System (NIDS)

NIDS monitors network traffic in real-time, analyzing packets as they traverse the network. It is typically deployed at strategic points within the network to inspect all inbound and outbound traffic. By analyzing network traffic patterns and comparing them against known threat signatures, NIDS can detect suspicious activities and generate alerts for administrators.

Host-Based Intrusion Detection System (HIDS)

HIDS focuses on monitoring activities on individual devices or hosts. It examines files, processes, and system logs for signs of compromise. HIDS is particularly effective in identifying insider threats and unauthorized changes to system configurations. By monitoring system-level activities, HIDS provides an additional layer of security, complementing the broader network-level monitoring provided by NIDS.

The key benefit of an IDS is its ability to provide early warning of potential security breaches. By continuously monitoring network traffic and system activities, IDS helps security teams identify and respond to threats before they escalate. However, it is important to note that IDS is a passive monitoring system, meaning it does not actively block or mitigate threats. Instead, it relies on security personnel to take appropriate action based on the alerts generated.

What is an IPS?

An IPS is a proactive security tool that not only detects threats but also takes immediate action to prevent them from compromising the network. Unlike IDS, which is passive, IPS operates inline with network traffic, actively monitoring and controlling the flow of data. When a threat is detected, IPS can automatically block, reroute, or quarantine malicious traffic, effectively preventing the attack from causing harm.

IPS can be implemented in various forms, including network-based IPS (NIPS) and host-based IPS (HIPS), similar to IDS. However, the primary distinction is that IPS takes immediate corrective actions to thwart potential threats.

Network-Based Intrusion Prevention System (NIPS)

NIPS is strategically placed within the network to monitor and control traffic in real-time. By analyzing traffic patterns and comparing them against predefined security policies and signatures, NIPS can block suspicious traffic, drop malicious packets, and even reset network connections if necessary. This proactive approach significantly reduces the risk of successful attacks and minimizes the impact of security incidents.

Host-Based Intrusion Prevention System (HIPS)

HIPS operates at the host level, monitoring and controlling processes and activities on individual devices. By enforcing security policies and preventing unauthorized changes to critical files and configurations, HIPS provides an additional layer of defense against insider threats and malware infections. HIPS can also block unauthorized applications and processes from executing, further enhancing the security posture of individual hosts.

The advantage of an IPS lies in its ability to provide real-time threat mitigation. By actively blocking and neutralizing threats, IPS helps organizations prevent security breaches and minimize the damage caused by cyberattacks. This proactive approach is particularly valuable in high-risk environments where rapid response to threats is essential.

Differences between IDS and IPS

While IDS and IPS share the common goal of protecting networks from threats, they differ significantly in their approach to achieving this objective. Understanding these differences is crucial for cybersecurity professionals to effectively deploy and manage these systems.

Detection vs. Prevention

An IDS is primarily focused on detection. It monitors network traffic and system activities to identify potential threats and generates alerts for administrators. IDS operates in a passive mode, meaning it does not take any direct action to block or mitigate threats. Instead, it relies on security personnel to respond to the alerts and take appropriate actions.

In contrast, an IPS is designed for prevention. It operates inline with network traffic, actively monitoring and controlling the flow of data. When a threat is detected, IPS can automatically block, reroute, or quarantine malicious traffic, effectively preventing the attack from causing harm. This proactive approach allows IPS to provide real-time threat mitigation.

Response Time

Since IDS is a passive monitoring system, its response time depends on the efficiency of security personnel in responding to alerts. The system itself does not take any immediate action to block threats, which means that there may be a delay in responding to security incidents.

Whereas, IPS being an active system, provides real-time threat mitigation. It can automatically block or neutralize threats as soon as they are detected, minimizing the impact of security incidents. This rapid response capability is a significant advantage in environments where timely threat mitigation is critical.

Placement and Deployment

IDS can be deployed at strategic points within the network to monitor traffic and system activities. It does not require inline placement, allowing for flexible deployment options. However, IDS relies on security personnel to take appropriate action based on the alerts generated.

Whereas, IPS must be deployed inline with network traffic to actively monitor and control data flow. This placement allows IPS to take immediate action to block or mitigate threats, but it may introduce latency and require careful planning to ensure network performance is not adversely affected.

Impact on Network Performance

Since IDS operates in a passive mode, it has minimal impact on network performance. It can analyze network traffic without introducing latency or affecting data flow. This makes IDS suitable for environments where network performance is a priority.

Whereas, IPS being an inline system, can introduce latency and affect network performance. The system must carefully analyze traffic in real-time, which may impact the overall speed and efficiency of data flow. Organizations must balance security and performance considerations when deploying IPS.

Successful Use-cases

The successful implementation of IDS and IPS has yielded significant benefits for organizations across various industries. These systems have become essential components of modern cybersecurity frameworks, helping organizations detect and prevent cyber threats effectively. Several companies have experienced remarkable success in enhancing their security posture by integrating IDS and IPS into their IT infrastructure. For instance, a leading financial institution implemented a comprehensive IDS and IPS solution to protect its sensitive customer data and financial transactions. By deploying a combination of network-based and host-based systems, the organization was able to monitor and control both network traffic and host-level activities. As a result, the financial institution significantly reduced the risk of data breaches and unauthorized access, safeguarding customer information and maintaining trust.

In another example, a global manufacturing company faced persistent cyber threats targeting its intellectual property and production systems. By implementing an advanced IDS and IPS solution, the organization achieved real-time threat detection and prevention capabilities. The system effectively blocked malicious traffic, prevented unauthorized access, and ensured the integrity of critical manufacturing processes. This proactive approach enabled the company to protect its valuable assets and maintain uninterrupted operations. Furthermore, a healthcare provider successfully leveraged IDS and IPS to comply with stringent regulatory requirements and protect patient data. By deploying a robust security infrastructure, the organization monitored network traffic for potential threats and prevented unauthorized access to patient records. This enhanced security posture not only ensured compliance but also instilled confidence in patients and stakeholders.

All these success stories highlight the transformative impact of IDS and IPS in enhancing cybersecurity defenses and mitigating the risk of cyberattacks. Organizations across diverse sectors have realized tangible benefits, including improved threat detection, rapid incident response, and enhanced data protection.

Introduction to Snort 3

Overview

Snort is a widely used open-source intrusion detection and prevention system (IDPS) that helps organizations detect and respond to security threats in real time. Originally developed by Martin Roesch in 1998, Snort has evolved into one of the most powerful and versatile tools in the cybersecurity landscape. It has a robust set of features that allow it to monitor network traffic, detect suspicious activities, and prevent malicious attacks. Snort operates by analyzing network packets and comparing them against a set of predefined rules and signatures to identify patterns indicative of cyber threats. This signature-based approach enables Snort to effectively detect known threats and block them before they can cause damage to the network.

Snort's architecture is highly modular, allowing it to be customized and extended to meet the specific needs of different organizations. It comprises several key components, including packet decoder, preprocessors, detection engine, and output modules. The packet decoder is responsible for capturing and normalizing network packets for analysis. Preprocessors perform various tasks, such as normalizing traffic, detecting anomalies, and reassembling fragmented packets. The detection engine is the core component that evaluates packets against the configured rules to identify potential threats. Finally, output modules handle alerting and logging, providing valuable information to security teams for further analysis and response.

Snort's flexibility and scalability make it suitable for a wide range of use cases, from small networks to large enterprise environments. It can be deployed as a standalone IDS or as part of a more comprehensive security infrastructure. Snort's ability to operate in different modes—such as sniffer mode, packet logger mode, and network intrusion detection mode—allows it to be tailored to specific security needs. Moreover, Snort can be integrated with other security tools and technologies, such as Security Information and Event Management (SIEM) systems, to enhance overall threat detection and response capabilities.

Snort's Impact on Healthcare Security

One compelling use case that highlights the impact of Snort in enhancing cybersecurity defenses is its deployment in the healthcare sector. Healthcare organizations are particularly vulnerable to cyber threats due to the sensitive nature of patient data and the increasing digitization of medical records. In this use case, a large healthcare provider implemented Snort as part of its cybersecurity strategy to protect patient information and maintain compliance with regulatory requirements such as the Health Insurance Portability and Accountability Act (HIPAA).

The healthcare provider faced several challenges, including the need to secure a diverse range of devices and systems, from electronic health records (EHR) systems to medical devices connected to the network. Additionally, the organization had to ensure that patient data remained confidential and protected against unauthorized access. By deploying Snort, the healthcare provider was able to gain real-time visibility into network traffic and identify potential threats before they could compromise sensitive information. Snort's ability to analyze network packets and detect anomalies played a crucial role in safeguarding patient data. The system monitored network traffic for suspicious activities, such as unauthorized access attempts, malware infections, and data exfiltration. Whenever a potential threat was detected, Snort generated alerts that were sent to the security operations center (SOC) for immediate investigation and response. This proactive approach enabled the healthcare provider to prevent data breaches and protect patient privacy.

Moreover, Snort's open-source nature allowed the healthcare provider to customize and fine-tune its detection rules to align with the organization's unique security requirements. The ability to create custom rules enabled the security team to detect specific threats targeting the healthcare sector, such as ransomware attacks and phishing attempts. Snort's flexibility and adaptability made it an invaluable tool in the organization's security arsenal, providing robust protection against evolving cyber threats. The deployment of Snort also facilitated compliance with HIPAA and other regulatory standards. By implementing an effective intrusion detection and prevention system, the healthcare provider demonstrated its commitment to safeguarding patient data and adhering to industry best practices. Snort's comprehensive logging and alerting capabilities provided the necessary documentation and audit trails required for compliance audits, further enhancing the organization's security posture.

Snort 3 Key Capabilities

Snort 3 represents a significant evolution in the capabilities and performance of the Snort platform. Building upon the strengths of its predecessors, Snort 3 introduces several enhancements that improve its effectiveness in detecting and preventing cyber threats. These key capabilities make Snort 3 a powerful and flexible tool for organizations seeking to bolster their cybersecurity defenses.

Enhanced Performance and Scalability

One of the standout features of Snort 3 is its improved performance and scalability. Snort 3 has been optimized to handle high-throughput environments, making it suitable for deployment in large enterprise networks. Its multithreaded architecture allows it to take advantage of modern hardware, distributing the workload across multiple CPU cores for faster packet processing. This enhancement significantly reduces the impact on network performance and enables Snort 3 to efficiently handle a higher volume of traffic.

Additionally, Snort 3 introduces support for hyperscan, an advanced regular expression matching library that accelerates pattern matching. This capability enhances the speed and accuracy of Snort's detection engine, allowing it to quickly identify threats and reduce false positives. With these performance improvements, organizations can deploy Snort 3 in high-traffic environments without sacrificing detection accuracy or network performance.

Modular and Extensible Architecture

Snort 3's modular architecture is a key factor in its flexibility and extensibility. The system is designed to be highly customizable, allowing organizations to tailor its functionality to meet their specific security needs. Snort 3 introduces the concept of "components," which are self-contained units that perform specific tasks within the system. Components can be easily added, removed, or modified, enabling organizations to adapt Snort 3 to evolving threats and changing network requirements.

Moreover, Snort 3 supports a wide range of preprocessors and plugins that extend its capabilities. These preprocessors can perform tasks such as traffic normalization, protocol analysis, and anomaly detection, enhancing Snort's ability to identify sophisticated attacks. The availability of third-party plugins further expands Snort's functionality, enabling organizations to integrate additional security features and technologies as needed.

Advanced Detection and Rule Management

Snort 3 introduces several enhancements to its detection and rule management capabilities. The detection engine has been optimized to support complex rule logic, allowing security teams to create more sophisticated rules that accurately detect advanced threats. Snort 3 supports various detection methodologies, including signature-based detection, anomaly-based detection, and behavior-based detection, providing a comprehensive approach to threat detection.

In addition, Snort 3 offers improved rule management capabilities that simplify the process of creating, updating, and organizing detection rules. The system supports rule sets that can be customized and fine-tuned to align with an organization's security policies and threat landscape. Snort 3 also introduces rule performance metrics, enabling security teams to evaluate the effectiveness of their rules and optimize them for better detection accuracy.

Integration with Security Ecosystem

Snort 3 is designed to seamlessly integrate with an organization's existing security ecosystem. The system supports various output formats, allowing it to send alerts and logs to external systems for further analysis and response. Snort 3 can be integrated with Security Information and Event Management (SIEM) systems, enabling centralized monitoring and correlation of security events. This integration enhances an organization's ability to detect and respond to threats in real time.

Furthermore, Snort 3 supports integration with threat intelligence feeds and reputation services, allowing it to leverage external threat data for improved threat detection. By incorporating threat intelligence into its detection engine, Snort 3 can identify emerging threats and provide actionable insights to security teams. This capability enhances an organization's ability to stay ahead of evolving cyber threats and proactively defend against attacks.

Community-Driven Development

One of the strengths of Snort is its vibrant and active community of users, developers, and security experts. Snort 3 continues to benefit from community-driven development, with contributions from a diverse group of individuals and organizations. The open-source nature of Snort allows the community to collaborate on improving the system, developing new features, and sharing threat intelligence.

This collaborative approach fosters innovation and ensures that Snort 3 remains at the forefront of intrusion detection and prevention technology. The community-driven development model also provides organizations with access to a wealth of resources, including rule sets, plugins, and best practices, enabling them to enhance their security defenses and respond effectively to emerging threats.

Preparing Linux with Snort and Dependencies

Before deploying Snort 3 as an IDPS, it's crucial to set up a robust Linux environment with all the necessary dependencies. This preparation ensures that Snort runs smoothly and efficiently, leveraging the full range of features available for threat detection and response. In this section, we will focus on configuring an Ubuntu system as our default operating environment, detailing the steps to install key dependencies required for Snort 3.

Installing Build Essentials

On your Ubuntu, open the terminal and run the following command to update your package list and upgrade existing packages:

```
sudo apt update && sudo apt upgrade -y
```

This command ensures your system is equipped with the latest software versions, enhancing overall security and performance. Then, we need to have the essential build tools installed on your system. These tools are necessary for compiling and building software from source. For this, run the following command:

```
sudo apt install build-essential -y
```

The build-essential package includes several key components, such as GCC (GNU Compiler Collection), G++ (GNU C++ Compiler), make (a utility for managing build processes), and additional development libraries needed for software compilation.

Installing Snort 3 Dependencies

Snort 3 requires a set of dependencies to function effectively as an IDPS. These dependencies provide essential functionality, such as packet capture, network utilities, scripting, and cryptography.

Now, we will explore the installation of each dependency in detail.

libdaq

Libdaq is a library that provides a unified interface for packet I/O, allowing Snort to capture network traffic efficiently. It supports various packet capture engines, including pcap, AFPacket, and netmap. To install libdaq, execute the following command:

```
sudo apt install libdaq-dev -y
```

This command installs the development package of libdaq, enabling Snort to leverage its packet I/O capabilities for real-time traffic analysis.

dnet

Dnet is a library that provides network utility functions for packet manipulation, including constructing and parsing network packets. It is used by Snort to interact with network protocols and manage packet data. Install dnet by running the following command:

```
sudo apt install libdnet-dev -y
```

With dnet installed, Snort can effectively analyze and manipulate network packets, supporting advanced threat detection and prevention techniques.

hwloc

Hwloc is a library that provides tools for managing CPU affinity and hardware locality, optimizing Snort's performance on multi-core systems. It allows Snort to bind processes to specific CPU cores, improving resource utilization and minimizing latency. Install hwloc using the following command:

```
sudo apt install libhwloc-dev -y
```

By leveraging hwloc, Snort can efficiently utilize system resources, enhancing its ability to handle high-throughput environments.

LuaJIT

LuaJIT is a Just-In-Time (JIT) compiler for the Lua scripting language, used by Snort for configuration and scripting purposes. It enables the creation of custom scripts and plugins to extend Snort's functionality. Install LuaJIT with the following command:

```
sudo apt install luajit -y
```

With LuaJIT, Snort can execute Lua scripts efficiently, enabling advanced threat detection and response capabilities through custom logic.

OpenSSL

OpenSSL is a cryptographic library that provides essential security functions, including encryption, decryption, and hashing. Snort uses OpenSSL for generating SHA and MD5 file signatures, facilitating the identification of malicious files and payloads. Install OpenSSL by executing the following command:

```
sudo apt install libssl-dev -y
```

The OpenSSL library enhances Snort's ability to perform cryptographic operations, contributing to the detection of threats that rely on encrypted communications.

pcap

Pcap (packet capture) is a library that provides an API for capturing and analyzing network traffic. It is widely used by network monitoring tools, including Snort, for capturing packets in real-time. Install pcap with the following command:

```
sudo apt install libpcap-dev -y
```

With pcap, Snort can capture network packets for analysis and logging, supporting the identification of suspicious activities and potential threats.

pcre

PCRE (Perl Compatible Regular Expressions) is a library that provides support for regular expression pattern matching, used by Snort to detect complex attack patterns and signatures. Install PCRE by executing the following command:

```
sudo apt install libpcre3-dev -y
```

The PCRE library enhances Snort's ability to match patterns within network traffic, enabling the detection of sophisticated and evasive threats.

pkg-config

Pkg-config is a tool that provides metadata about installed libraries, helping to locate build dependencies required by software projects. It simplifies the process of compiling and linking libraries during the build process. Install pkg-config with the following command:

```
sudo apt install pkg-config -y
```

By using pkg-config, Snort can efficiently manage its build dependencies, ensuring a smooth compilation and installation process.

zlib

Zlib is a compression library that provides support for data compression and decompression, used by Snort to handle compressed network traffic and payloads. Install zlib with the following command:

```
sudo apt install zlib1g-dev -y
```

The zlib library enables Snort to process compressed data, allowing it to analyze network traffic that utilizes compression techniques.

Compiling and Installing Snort 3

With all the necessary dependencies installed from the previous section, you can now proceed to compile and install Snort 3. See the below steps:

Download Snort 3 Source Code

Begin by downloading the Snort 3 source code from the official Snort website or GitHub repository. You can use the following commands to download and extract the source code:

```
wget
https://github.com/snort3/snort3/archive/refs/tags/3.1.50
.0.tar.gz

tar -xvzf 3.1.50.0.tar.gz

cd snort3-3.1.50.0
```

Replace **`3.1.50.0`** with the latest version number available at the time of download.

Configure Snort Build

Run the **`./configure`** script to configure the build process. This script checks for the necessary dependencies and sets up the build environment. You can include additional options as needed, such as enabling specific features or components:

```
./configure --enable-sourcefire --enable-debug
```

The **`--enable-sourcefire`** option enables Sourcefire-specific features, while **`--`**

enable-debug enables debugging options for troubleshooting.

Compile and Install Snort

After configuring the build, use the **make** command to compile Snort. This process may take some time, depending on your system's performance:

```
make
```

Once the compilation is complete, install Snort using the **make install** command:

```
sudo make install
```

This command installs Snort and its components in the appropriate directories, making it ready for use.

Verify Snort

To verify that Snort has been installed successfully, run the following command to check the version:

```
snort --version
```

The output should display the installed version of Snort, confirming that the installation was successful.

Setup Snort Configuration Files

Snort's operation is guided by its configuration files, which define its behavior and detection rules. Create a directory for Snort configuration files and copy the default configuration files from the source directory:

```
sudo mkdir /etc/snort

sudo cp etc/*.conf /etc/snort/
```

These configuration files include **snort.conf**, which is the main configuration file where you define network variables, configure preprocessors, and specify detection rules.

Test Snort Configuration

Before deploying Snort in a production environment, it's important to test its configuration to ensure it's functioning correctly. Run Snort in test mode using the following command:

```
sudo snort -T -c /etc/snort/snort.conf
```

The **-T** option runs Snort in test mode, verifying the configuration file for errors. Review the output for any warnings or errors and make necessary adjustments to the configuration. With Snort 3 now successfully installed, you are now ready to proceed with configuring its detection rules and integrating it into your security infrastructure.

Setting up a Virtual Lab

Creating a virtual lab is a vital step in experimenting with Snort 3 for intrusion detection and prevention without affecting live systems. A virtual lab provides a controlled environment where you can safely test network configurations, simulate attacks, and observe Snort's response. This topic will take you through setting up a virtual machine named **GitforGits machine** and configuring a star topology that will be used throughout the book for practical learning.

Creating a Virtual Machine

To start, we will create a virtual machine using VirtualBox, a popular open-source virtualization software. VirtualBox allows you to run multiple operating systems on your host machine, providing a sandboxed environment for testing and development. If you haven't already installed VirtualBox, download and install it from the official website.

Following are the steps to create a virtual machine:

- Launch VirtualBox and click on the "New" button to create a new virtual machine. This will open the "Create Virtual Machine" wizard.
- Enter the name **GitforGits machine** for the virtual machine. Select **Linux** as the operating system type. Choose **Ubuntu (64-bit)** from the dropdown list.
- Allocate memory for the virtual machine. A minimum of **2 GB (2048 MB)** is recommended, but you can allocate more if your host system has sufficient RAM.
- Choose the option **"Create a virtual hard disk now"** and click **"Create."**
- Select **VDI (VirtualBox Disk Image)** as the hard disk file type and click **"Next."**
- Choose **"Dynamically allocated"** to allow the virtual disk to grow as needed and click **"Next."**
- Specify the location where the virtual disk file will be stored. Allocate at least **20 GB** for the virtual disk to ensure there is enough space for Snort and its dependencies.
- Click **"Create"** to finalize the creation of the GitforGits machine. The virtual machine will now appear in the VirtualBox Manager.

Installing Ubuntu on Virtual Machine

With the GitforGits machine created, the next step is to install Ubuntu. Download the Ubuntu Server ISO file from the official Ubuntu website. After that, carry out the following steps to install Ubuntu:

- Select the GitforGits machine in the VirtualBox Manager and click the **"Start"** button. When prompted, choose the Ubuntu Server ISO file as the startup disk.
- Follow the on-screen instructions to install Ubuntu Server on the virtual machine. The installation process involves selecting your language, keyboard layout, and time zone. You'll also need to configure a username and password for the system.
- During the installation, you'll be prompted to select software packages. Choose the option to install **OpenSSH server** to enable remote access to the virtual machine.
- Once the installation is complete, remove the installation media and restart the virtual machine. You should now have a fully functional Ubuntu Server running on the GitforGits machine.

Configuring a Star Topology

A star topology is a network configuration where all devices are connected to a central hub or switch, allowing for easy management and scalability. In our virtual lab, we will configure a star topology with the GitforGits machine acting as one of the nodes. This topology will facilitate testing Snort's capabilities in a simulated network environment.

The below are the steps to configure a star topology:

- To simulate a star topology, we will create additional virtual machines to act as nodes in the network. Follow the same steps as above to create two more virtual machines, naming them **Node1** and **Node2.**
- Install Ubuntu Server on Node1 and Node2, following the same installation process used for the GitforGits machine. Ensure that each virtual machine is configured with a unique hostname.
- We will use VirtualBox's internal network feature to connect all virtual machines in a star topology. This configuration allows the VMs to communicate with each other while being isolated from the host machine and external networks.
- Open the settings for each virtual machine (GitforGits, Node1, Node2) and navigate to the "Network" tab. Set the adapter type to **"Internal Network"** and ensure all VMs are part of the same internal network, e.g., **"LabNetwork."**
- Then, log in to each virtual machine and edit the network configuration file to assign static IP addresses. For Ubuntu Server, this can be done by editing the netplan configuration file.

For example,

- edit **/etc/netplan/00-installer-config.yaml** on each VM:

```
network:
  ethernets:
    enp0s3:
      dhcp4: no
      addresses:
        - 192.168.56.101/24  # GitforGits IP
  version: 2
```

- Update the IP addresses for each VM as follows:
  - GitforGits: **192.168.56.101**
  - Node1: **192.168.56.102**
  - Node2: **192.168.56.103**
- Apply the changes using the **netplan apply** command.

In a physical network, a star topology would include a central hub or switch. In our virtual lab, the GitforGits machine will serve as the central hub, responsible for monitoring network traffic and managing connections between nodes.

On the GitforGits machine, install bridge utilities to enable network bridging:

```
sudo apt install bridge-utils -y
```

Then, edit the netplan configuration file on the GitforGits machine to create a network bridge that connects all nodes in the star topology. Add the following configuration:

```
network:
  version: 2
  ethernets:
```

```
    enp0s3:
      dhcp4: no
  bridges:
    br0:
      dhcp4: no
      interfaces:
        - enp0s3
      addresses:
        - 192.168.56.101/24
```

Apply the changes using the **netplan apply** command. Now, with the star topology configured, test connectivity between the virtual machines to ensure they can communicate with each other. Use the **ping** command from one VM to another:

```
ping 192.168.56.102   # From GitforGits to Node1
ping 192.168.56.103   # From GitforGits to Node2
```

As you proceed with setting up your virtual lab, you may find it helpful to install additional tools on the virtual machines to facilitate testing and experimentation. These tools include network analyzers, packet generators, and traffic simulators, which can be used to create realistic network scenarios for Snort testing.

- **Wireshark**

A popular network analyzer that provides detailed insights into network traffic. Install Wireshark on the GitforGits machine to analyze packets captured by Snort:

```
sudo apt install wireshark -y
```

- **Hping3**

A packet generator and network testing tool that allows you to create custom packets for testing Snort's detection capabilities. Install hping3 on the GitforGits machine:

```
sudo apt install hping3 -y
```

- **Netcat**

A versatile networking tool used for debugging and testing network connections. Install netcat on all virtual machines:

```
sudo apt install netcat -y
```

Simulating Network Traffic

With the virtual lab set up, you can now simulate network traffic to test Snort's intrusion detection and prevention capabilities. Use hping3 to generate various types of network traffic and observe how Snort detects and responds to potential threats.

Generating ICMP Traffic

Use hping3 to send ICMP echo requests (ping) from Node1 to GitforGits:

```
hping3 -1 192.168.56.101 -c 10  # Sends 10 ICMP echo
requests
```

Monitor the traffic on the GitforGits machine using Wireshark or Snort to verify that the packets are being captured and analyzed.

Simulating a TCP SYN Flood Attack

Use hping3 to simulate a TCP SYN flood attack from Node2 to GitforGits:

```
hping3 -S 192.168.56.101 -p 80 --flood  # Sends a flood
of TCP SYN packets to port 80
```

Observe Snort's response to the simulated attack and assess the alerts generated. This exercise demonstrates Snort's ability to detect and respond to potential threats in real-time.

The virtual lab you've set up will serve as a consistent environment for testing and experimenting with Snort throughout the book. And, as you progress through subsequent chapters, you can use this lab to explore advanced topics, configure detection rules, and simulate various attack scenarios.

Security and Ethical Considerations

The field of cybersecurity is governed by numerous laws and ethical principles designed to protect privacy, maintain data integrity, and prevent unauthorized access. Understanding and following these guidelines is crucial for any cybersecurity professional to avoid legal repercussions and uphold the ethical standards of the industry. This section will cover the key legal and ethical considerations when working with Snort and performing IDPS operations, and also propose best practices to ensure safe and compliant testing.

Legal Guidelines for Performing IDPS Operations

Cybersecurity operations, including the use of intrusion detection and prevention systems like Snort, are subject to various legal requirements and regulations. These laws are designed to safeguard sensitive information, protect individual privacy, and maintain the integrity of IT systems. Failing to adhere to these legal guidelines can result in significant penalties, including fines, legal actions, and damage to reputation.

Data Protection and Privacy Laws

One of the primary legal considerations when working with Snort is compliance with data protection and privacy laws. These laws govern the collection, processing, and storage of personal data and vary by jurisdiction. In the United States, several federal and state laws apply to data privacy, including the Health Insurance Portability and Accountability Act (HIPAA), the California Consumer Privacy Act (CCPA), and the Gramm-Leach-Bliley Act (GLBA). In the European Union, the General Data Protection Regulation (GDPR) is a comprehensive privacy law that mandates strict data protection requirements.

When deploying Snort or performing IDPS operations, it's crucial to ensure that your activities comply with applicable data protection and privacy laws. This includes obtaining consent for monitoring network traffic, anonymizing or pseudonymizing personal data, and implementing appropriate security measures to protect data from unauthorized access or disclosure.

Computer Fraud and Abuse Act (CFAA)

The Computer Fraud and Abuse Act (CFAA) is a United States federal law that prohibits unauthorized access to computers and networks. It criminalizes activities such as hacking, distributing malware, and exceeding authorized access to computer systems. When using Snort for IDPS operations, it's essential to ensure that you have proper authorization to monitor and analyze network traffic. Unauthorized use of Snort or other IDPS tools can result in violations of the CFAA and lead to severe legal consequences.

Electronic Communications Privacy Act (ECPA)

The Electronic Communications Privacy Act (ECPA) is another key legal framework in the

United States that regulates the interception and disclosure of electronic communications. The ECPA prohibits unauthorized interception of wire, oral, and electronic communications, including emails and network traffic. When using Snort to capture and analyze network packets, ensure that your activities comply with the ECPA and any applicable state laws governing electronic communications.

Compliance with Industry Regulations

Many industries are subject to specific regulations that mandate security requirements for protecting sensitive data. For example, the financial sector is governed by regulations such as the Payment Card Industry Data Security Standard (PCI DSS) and the Sarbanes-Oxley Act (SOX). The healthcare industry must comply with HIPAA, while government agencies are subject to the Federal Information Security Management Act (FISMA). When implementing Snort and performing IDPS operations, it's essential to align your activities with relevant industry regulations to ensure compliance and avoid potential legal and financial penalties.

Ethical Guidelines for Performing IDPS Operations

In addition to legal requirements, cybersecurity professionals are expected to adhere to ethical guidelines that promote integrity, responsibility, and accountability in their work. Ethical considerations are essential for maintaining trust and upholding the principles of cybersecurity.

Respect for Privacy

Respecting individual privacy is a fundamental ethical principle in cybersecurity. When using Snort to monitor network traffic, it's important to minimize the collection and analysis of personal data and ensure that any data collected is used solely for legitimate security purposes. Avoid accessing or disclosing sensitive information without proper authorization, and implement measures to protect the privacy of individuals whose data may be captured during IDPS operations.

Transparency and Accountability

Transparency and accountability are critical components of ethical cybersecurity practices. Ensure that stakeholders, including employees and customers, are informed about the use of IDPS tools like Snort and the purposes of monitoring network traffic. Establish clear policies and procedures for handling security incidents and ensure that security operations are conducted with transparency and accountability.

Professionalism and Integrity

Cybersecurity professionals are expected to demonstrate professionalism and integrity in their work. This includes adhering to industry standards and best practices, continuously updating skills and knowledge, and conducting security operations with honesty and integrity. Avoid engaging in activities that could compromise the security or integrity of IT systems, and report any unethical behavior or security vulnerabilities to appropriate authorities.

Avoidance of Harm

A key ethical consideration in cybersecurity is the avoidance of harm to individuals, organizations, and society as a whole. When using Snort and performing IDPS operations, ensure that your actions do not cause unnecessary harm or disruption to network services. Implement measures to prevent false positives and false negatives, and ensure that security incidents are handled promptly and effectively to minimize potential harm.

Best Practices for Safe Testing

While conducting cybersecurity operations and testing Snort's capabilities, it's essential to implement best practices that ensure safe and effective testing. These practices not only enhance the security of your environment but also promote ethical and compliant operations.

Use a Controlled Environment

Conduct testing in a controlled environment, such as a virtual lab or test network, to prevent unintended consequences on production systems. Isolate the test environment from live networks to avoid disruptions and minimize the risk of data breaches. By using a controlled environment, you can safely test Snort's capabilities, simulate attacks, and observe its response without impacting real users or systems.

Obtain Proper Authorization

Ensure that you have proper authorization to conduct IDPS operations and monitor network traffic. Obtain consent from network owners and stakeholders before deploying Snort and conducting tests. Clearly define the scope of testing and ensure that all activities are authorized and documented.

Anonymize and Protect Data

Implement measures to anonymize or pseudonymize personal data collected during IDPS operations. Use encryption and access controls to protect sensitive data from unauthorized access or disclosure. Ensure that data is used only for legitimate security purposes and that privacy rights are respected throughout the testing process.

Document and Review Security Operations

Document all security operations and testing activities, including the configuration of Snort, the types of attacks simulated, and the results of tests. Regularly review and update documentation to reflect changes in the security environment. Conduct post-testing reviews to evaluate the effectiveness of IDPS operations and identify areas for improvement.

Collaborate with Stakeholders

Engage stakeholders in the testing process and collaborate with IT teams, management, and other relevant parties to ensure alignment with organizational goals and objectives. Provide regular updates on security operations and testing activities, and seek input from stakeholders to improve security practices and address potential concerns.

By ensuring compliance with data protection laws, respecting individual privacy, and promoting transparency and accountability are key components of responsible cybersecurity operations. As you continue to explore Snort's capabilities, these considerations will help you conduct IDPS operations with integrity and professionalism, contributing to a more secure and resilient digital environment.

Summary

This chapter provided an overview of IDS and IPS, outlining the basic ideas behind these systems and highlighting their pivotal role in keeping networks secure. The difference between IPS and IDS was explained to you. IDS merely watched network traffic for possible threats, while IPS actively blocked them. The differences between these systems demonstrated the significance of both detection and prevention in maintaining a secure network. The chapter also provided an overview of Snort 3, a powerful open-source tool for IDS/IPS operations, including its architecture and features.

The section on preparing a Linux environment walked you through the installation of necessary dependencies on Ubuntu to ensure Snort's proper operation. The installation of libraries like OpenSSL for cryptographic functions, dnet for network utilities, and libdaq for packet I/O were all part of this setup process. You then learned how to set up a virtual lab with VirtualBox, including a star topology with the GitforGits machine and additional nodes for practical testing. The chapter concluded with a discussion of security and ethical considerations, including data protection laws, privacy, and the importance of obtaining proper authorization. The chapter recommended best practices for safe testing, such as using controlled environments and anonymizing data, to ensure that you understood how to conduct security operations responsibly and ethically.

Chapter 2: Installing and Configuring Snort 3

Chapter Overview

In Chapter 2, we will explore how to install and configure Snort 3 in order to implement its powerful IDS/IPS capabilities. This chapter is meant to walk you through the process of configuring Snort 3 on Linux, making sure it's tailor-made for your network security requirements. You'll start by learning how to configure Snort 3, including how to tailor its settings and rules to effectively detect potential threats.

Following the configuration, you'll learn how to integrate Snort with Barnyard2 and BASE, two tools that extend Snort's capabilities. Barnyard2 serves as a critical intermediary, processing Snort output and efficiently handling log data, whereas BASE provides a simple interface for monitoring and analyzing security alerts. Once you have a good grasp of these integrations, you'll be able to simplify alert management and elevate visibility into network activity in general. After you've configured Snort and its supporting tools, you will go over essential testing techniques, such as simulating attacks and monitoring Snort's response to ensure its effectiveness. By mastering these testing methods, you will be able to validate Snort's configuration and ensure that it correctly detects and reports threats in your network. This hands-on approach not only reinforces your understanding of Snort's capabilities, but also boosts your confidence in your ability to run a reliable IDS.

The chapter then concludes with addressing common installation and configuration issues, as well as practical troubleshooting techniques for potential problems. This section will go over various scenarios, such as dependency conflicts, configuration errors, and performance issues, and provide solutions to keep your Snort deployment reliable and efficient. By learning to troubleshoot effectively, you will be better prepared to deal with any issues that may arise, ensuring Snort continues to function optimally in your security infrastructure.

Configuring Snort 3

Configuring Snort 3 involves understanding and interacting with its configuration files, which dictate how Snort analyzes network traffic and responds to potential threats. These files contain various settings and rules that define Snort's behavior, enabling it to detect and prevent security incidents. In this section, we will explore Snort's configuration files and take you through performing basic configuration settings to get Snort up and running in your network environment.

Understanding Snort Configuration Files

Snort 3's configuration system is organized around several key files and directories. These files contain information on network variables, preprocessors, detection rules, and output settings.

Here, we will explore the primary configuration files and their purposes:

snort.lua

The **snort.lua** file is the main configuration file in Snort 3. Unlike previous versions of Snort, which used a text-based configuration file (**snort.conf**), Snort 3 uses a Lua script for configuration. This change allows for more flexibility and programmability in setting up Snort.

The **snort.lua** file contains various sections, each responsible for different aspects of Snort's configuration, such as network settings, rule paths, and output modules.

classification.config

The **classification.config** file defines the classification of alerts generated by Snort. It maps specific alert types to descriptive categories, making it easier for security personnel to understand the nature of detected threats. For example, a rule that detects a port scan might generate an alert classified as "recon," while a rule that detects malware activity might generate an alert classified as "malware."

reference.config

The **reference.config** file provides references to external resources for alerts generated by Snort. It links specific alerts to documentation, CVE entries, or other relevant sources of information. This file helps security analysts quickly access additional details about detected threats, enabling more informed decision-making during incident response.

threshold.config

The **threshold.config** file allows you to define thresholds and suppressions for specific rules. This configuration file helps manage alert noise by specifying conditions under which alerts should be generated, limited, or suppressed. By configuring thresholds, you can reduce false positives and focus on the most critical threats.

rules directory

The **rules** directory contains individual rule files, each specifying patterns and conditions for detecting specific threats. Snort 3 supports various rule types, including signature-based rules, protocol-specific rules, and custom rules. The rules directory is organized into subdirectories, allowing for easy management of rulesets.

Interacting with Snort Configuration Files

To configure Snort, you'll need to edit the configuration files to specify network settings, enable preprocessors, define detection rules, and configure output options. This process involves using a text editor, such as **nano** or **vim**, to modify the contents of these files.

Open a terminal and navigate to the directory where Snort's configuration files are stored. By default, this directory is typically located at **/etc/snort/**.

```
cd /etc/snort/
```

Use a text editor to open the **snort.lua** file for editing.

```
sudo nano /etc/snort/snort.lua
```

You can also use **vim** or any other text editor of your choice:

```
sudo vim /etc/snort/snort.lua
```

In addition to the **snort.lua** file, you may need to access and edit other configuration files, such as **classification.config** and **threshold.config**, depending on your specific requirements.

Performing Basic Configuration Settings

With access to the configuration files, you can now perform basic configuration settings to customize Snort for your network environment. These settings include defining network variables, enabling preprocessors, specifying rule paths, and configuring output modules.

Define Network Variables

Network variables allow Snort to identify and differentiate between trusted and untrusted network segments. By defining these variables, you can tailor Snort's detection rules to your specific network topology.

In the **snort.lua** file, locate the section that defines network variables. You'll typically find variables for internal networks, external networks, and server addresses. Modify these variables to match your network configuration.

```
HOME_NET = '192.168.1.0/24'  -- Define your internal
network range

EXTERNAL_NET = '!$HOME_NET'  -- Define the external
network as anything outside the internal range
```

The **HOME_NET** variable represents your internal network, while the **EXTERNAL_NET** variable represents networks that are not part of your internal range. Adjust these variables to reflect your network's IP addressing scheme.

Enable Preprocessors

Preprocessors are modules that analyze network traffic and perform tasks such as normalization, decoding, and anomaly detection. Enabling preprocessors enhances Snort's ability to detect complex threats.

In the **snort.lua** file, locate the section for preprocessors and enable the ones relevant to your network environment. For example, you can enable the **stream** preprocessor for TCP stream reassembly and the **frag3** preprocessor for IP fragmentation handling.

```
stream = { }

frag3 = { }
```

Preprocessors can be configured with additional options, such as timeout settings and buffer sizes. Consult the Snort documentation for details on configuring specific preprocessors.

Specify Rule Paths

Snort relies on rule files to detect specific threats. You need to specify the paths to these rule files in the **snort.lua** file, ensuring that Snort can access and apply them during analysis.

In the **snort.lua** file, locate the section for rule paths and specify the directories where your rule files are stored. You can use the default rule paths or customize them based on your directory structure.

```
rules = [[

    include $RULE_PATH/local.rules

    include $RULE_PATH/community.rules

    include $RULE_PATH/snort3-core.rules

]]
```

The **rules** variable lists the rule files that Snort will load during startup. Ensure that these files exist in the specified directories and contain valid detection rules.

Configure Output Modules

Output modules determine how Snort logs alerts and other data. Configuring these modules allows you to specify the format and destination of Snort's output, such as logging to a file, sending alerts to a database, or forwarding events to a SIEM system.

In the **snort.lua** file, locate the section for output modules and configure the desired output options. For example, you can enable logging to a unified2 file or send alerts to syslog.

```
alert_fast = { file = true }
```

The **alert_fast** option logs alerts to a file in a human-readable format, while the **alert_syslog** option sends alerts to syslog for centralized logging. Customize the output modules based on your organization's logging and alerting requirements.

Save and Exit

After making the necessary changes to the configuration files, save your modifications and exit the text editor. For **nano**, press **Ctrl + O** to save and **Ctrl + X** to exit. For **vim**, press **Esc**, then type **:wq** and hit **Enter** to save and exit.

```
# In nano:

# Press Ctrl + O, then Enter to save changes

# Press Ctrl + X to exit the editor



# In vim:

# Press Esc, then type :wq and press Enter to save
changes and exit
```

Restart Snort

To apply the configuration changes, restart the Snort service. This step ensures that Snort loads the updated configuration and rules.

```
sudo systemctl restart snort
```

Alternatively, if you are running Snort manually, stop and restart the Snort process with the updated configuration.

```
sudo snort -c /etc/snort/snort.lua
```

This command runs Snort with the specified configuration file (**snort.lua**), applying the settings and rules defined in the file.

Verify Configuration

It's important to verify that Snort is running with the correct configuration and is capable of detecting network traffic.

To do this,

- check Snort's logs and output files to ensure that it's operating as expected. Review the log files in the **/var/log/snort/** directory to confirm that Snort is capturing network events and generating alerts.
- Use tools like **tail** or **cat** to view the logs in real-time.

```
tail -f /var/log/snort/alert
```

This command displays the latest alerts in the **alert** log file, allowing you to monitor Snort's activity and verify its effectiveness.

Testing Snort Installation

Once Snort is installed and configured, the next step is to test its functionality to ensure it operates correctly as an IDS. Testing Snort involves running it in IDS mode, simulating attacks, and verifying that it accurately detects and alerts on potential threats. This section will take you through the process of testing Snort's capabilities, ensuring that all features and functionalities are working as expected.

Running Snort in IDS Mode

Snort operates in three main modes: sniffer mode, packet logger mode, and network intrusion detection mode (IDS mode). In IDS mode, Snort analyzes network traffic in real-time, detecting and alerting on suspicious activities based on predefined rules. Here, we will begin by running Snort in IDS mode.

Start Snort in IDS Mode

To start Snort in IDS mode, you'll need to use the **-c** option to specify the configuration file and the **-i** option to specify the network interface you want to monitor. Open a terminal and run the following command:

```
sudo snort -c /etc/snort/snort.lua -i eth0
```

Replace **eth0** with the appropriate network interface name for your system. You can use the **ip a** command to list network interfaces and identify the correct one. This command launches Snort with the specified configuration file (**snort.lua**) and monitors traffic on the specified network interface in IDS mode.

Monitor Snort Output

As Snort runs in IDS mode, it will analyze network traffic and generate alerts for any suspicious activities it detects. By default, Snort logs alerts to the **/var/log/snort/alert** file. Use the **tail** command to monitor the alerts in real-time:

```
sudo tail -f /var/log/snort/alert
```

The **tail** command continuously displays the latest entries in the alert log, allowing you to observe Snort's detection capabilities and verify that it's functioning as expected.

Testing Simulated Attacks

To effectively test Snort's installation, it's essential to simulate various attack scenarios and verify that Snort accurately detects and alerts on them. Now, we will explore how to simulate different types of attacks and assess Snort's capabilities.

Simulating a Port Scan

Port scans are common reconnaissance techniques used by attackers to identify open ports and services on a network. To simulate a port scan, we will use the **nmap** tool from one of the virtual machines in your lab environment.

If **nmap** is not already installed on one of your virtual machines (e.g., Node1), install it using the following command:

```
sudo apt install nmap -y
```

Run a port scan from Node1 targeting the GitforGits machine's IP address:

```
nmap -sS 192.168.56.101
```

This command initiates a SYN scan (**-sS**), which is a stealthy method of scanning for open ports. Then, monitor the alert log on the GitforGits machine to verify that Snort detects the port scan and generates alerts. You should see alerts indicating a potential reconnaissance activity, reflecting Snort's ability to identify scanning attempts.

Simulating a Ping Flood Attack

A ping flood attack is a type of denial-of-service (DoS) attack that overwhelms a target system with ICMP echo requests (pings). To simulate a ping flood attack, we will use the **hping3** tool from Node2.

If **hping3** is not already installed on Node2, install it using the following command:

```
sudo apt install hping3 -y
```

Use **hping3** to send a flood of ICMP echo requests to the GitforGits machine:

```
hping3 --flood --icmp 192.168.56.101
```

The **--flood** option sends packets as fast as possible, simulating a DoS attack.

Testing Rule-Based Detection

Snort's detection capabilities rely on a set of predefined rules that specify patterns and conditions for identifying threats. To test rule-based detection, we will create a custom rule that triggers an alert when a specific string is detected in network traffic.

For this, edit the **local.rules** file in the Snort rules directory and add a custom rule:

```
sudo nano /etc/snort/rules/local.rules
```

Add the following rule to the file:

```
alert tcp any any -> any any (msg:"Test Alert: Detected
custom string"; content:"customstring"; sid:1000001;
rev:1;)
```

This rule generates an alert when it detects the string "customstring" in TCP traffic.

Save the changes to the **local.rules** file and restart Snort to apply the new rule:

```
sudo systemctl restart snort
```

Use **netcat** on Node1 to send a TCP packet containing the custom string to the GitforGits machine:

```
echo "customstring" | nc 192.168.56.101 12345
```

This test demonstrates Snort's ability to detect user-defined patterns in network traffic.

Verifying Snort's Features and Capabilities

In the previous chapter, we explored several features and capabilities of Snort, including preprocessors, output modules, and logging. Now, we will verify these functionalities to ensure Snort is configured and operating correctly.

Testing Preprocessors

Preprocessors enhance Snort's detection capabilities by analyzing network traffic and performing various tasks such as normalization and anomaly detection. Verify that preprocessors are functioning as expected by assessing their output and behavior.

The **stream** preprocessor is responsible for TCP stream reassembly, enabling Snort to analyze complete sessions rather than individual packets. Verify its functionality by assessing alerts related to fragmented or incomplete TCP streams.

Simulate a fragmented TCP session from Node1:

```
hping3 -c 1 -d 50 -S -p 80 --frag 192.168.56.101
```

Check the alert log to ensure Snort generates alerts for fragmented packets, indicating the **stream** preprocessor is functioning correctly.

The **http_inspect** preprocessor analyzes HTTP traffic to detect web-based threats. Verify its functionality by simulating HTTP traffic with potentially malicious content.

From Node1, send an HTTP request with a suspicious user-agent string:

```
echo -e "GET / HTTP/1.1\r\nHost: gitforgits.com\r\nUser-
Agent: MaliciousAgent\r\n\r\n" | nc 192.168.56.101 80
```

Check the alert log for alerts related to suspicious HTTP traffic, confirming the **http_inspect** preprocessor is working as intended.

Testing Output Modules

Snort's output modules determine how alerts and logs are recorded and reported. Verify the functionality of the configured output modules by examining the logs and alerts generated during testing.

If Snort is configured to use the unified2 output module, verify that alerts are logged in the unified2 format. Check the **/var/log/snort** directory for unified2 files.

```
ls /var/log/snort/
```

Ensure that unified2 log files are being created and updated, indicating the output module is functioning correctly.

If Snort is configured to send alerts to syslog, verify that alerts are being forwarded to the system's syslog service. Use the **journalctl** command to view syslog entries related to Snort:

```
sudo journalctl -u snort
```

Check for alert entries in the syslog output, confirming that Snort is successfully integrating with the syslog service.

Testing Logging and Alerting

Logging and alerting are crucial components of Snort's functionality, providing visibility into network events and security incidents. Verify that Snort is accurately logging and alerting on detected threats.

Assess the alert log file to ensure that alerts are being generated for each simulated attack and custom rule. Verify that the log entries include relevant information, such as source and destination IP addresses, port numbers, and alert messages.

```
sudo cat /var/log/snort/alert
```

If Snort is configured to capture packets, review the packet capture logs to ensure that network traffic is being recorded accurately. Use tools like **tcpdump** or **Wireshark** to analyze the captured packets.

```
sudo tcpdump -r /var/log/snort/snort.log.<timestamp>
```

Analyze the packet capture to confirm that Snort is correctly capturing and logging network traffic for analysis.

By running test cases that mimic real-world attacks (e.g., port scans, denial-of-service attacks, and custom rule-based detections), you can make sure that Snort is an effective intrusion detection system (IDS). You can also check that Snort's features and capabilities (e.g., preprocessors, output modules, and logging) work as expected in your network environment.

Troubleshooting Installation Issues

Installing Snort 3 and its dependencies can be complex due to the various components and configurations involved. While following the installation steps, you may encounter several potential issues. This section will cover common issues you might encounter during the installation and configuration of Snort and its dependencies, along with solutions to address these challenges.

Common Installation Issues

Missing or Outdated Dependencies

One of the most common issues during installation is missing or outdated dependencies. Snort relies on several libraries and tools, such as libdaq, libdnet, and LuaJIT, which must be correctly installed and up-to-date.

To overcome it, verify that all required dependencies are installed. Use package managers like **apt** to check for installed packages and their versions:

```
dpkg -l | grep -E 'libdaq|libdnet|luajit'
```

If a dependency is missing or outdated, install or update it using the package manager:

```
sudo apt install libdaq-dev libdnet-dev luajit
```

Ensure that the correct versions are installed, as Snort may have specific version requirements for certain libraries.

Configuration File Errors

Configuration file errors can occur if there are syntax mistakes or incorrect settings in the Snort configuration files. These errors can prevent Snort from starting correctly or functioning as expected.

To resolve this, review the Snort configuration files (**snort.lua**, **classification.config**, etc.) for syntax errors or incorrect settings. Use a text editor with syntax highlighting, such as **vim**, to help identify mistakes.

```
sudo vim /etc/snort/snort.lua
```

Run Snort in test mode to validate the configuration file and identify any errors:

```
sudo snort -T -c /etc/snort/snort.lua
```

The output will display any configuration errors or warnings. Address these issues by correcting the configuration files based on the error messages.

Network Interface Issues

Snort requires access to a network interface to capture and analyze traffic. Issues may arise if

Snort is unable to bind to the specified interface or if the interface is misconfigured.

In this, first verify that the correct network interface is specified in the Snort command. Use the **ip a** command to list available interfaces and identify the correct one:

```
ip a
```

Ensure that the network interface is up and running. Use the **ip link set** command to bring the interface up if necessary:

```
sudo ip link set eth0 up
```

Check for permission issues that may prevent Snort from accessing the interface. Ensure that Snort is run with sufficient privileges (e.g., using **sudo**) to capture traffic.

Permission Denied Errors

Permission issues can prevent Snort from accessing required files or directories, leading to errors during startup or operation.

To avoid such errors, verify the permissions of Snort's configuration files and log directories. Use the **ls -l** command to check ownership and permissions:

```
ls -l /etc/snort/

ls -l /var/log/snort/
```

Ensure that Snort runs with appropriate permissions. Use **sudo** to execute Snort commands and access restricted files:

```
sudo snort -c /etc/snort/snort.lua -i eth0
```

If running Snort as a non-root user, configure the necessary permissions for that user to access network interfaces and log directories.

Library Path Issues

Library path issues can occur if Snort or its dependencies are not correctly installed or if the library paths are misconfigured.

To address this issue, first verify the library paths using the **ldd** command to check for missing or misconfigured libraries:

```
ldd $(which snort)
```

If a library is missing or not found, update the library path using the **LD_LIBRARY_PATH** environment variable:

```
export LD_LIBRARY_PATH=/usr/local/lib:$LD_LIBRARY_PATH
```

Reinstall any missing libraries and ensure they are correctly linked to the library path:

```
sudo ldconfig
```

Snort Crashing or Not Starting

Snort may crash or fail to start if there are conflicts with other processes or if the system resources are insufficient.

In this, check for conflicting processes using the same network interface or ports. Use the **netstat** command to identify active connections:

```
sudo netstat -tuln
```

Stop any conflicting processes or services that may interfere with Snort's operation. Then, verify that the system meets the resource requirements for running Snort, such as CPU, memory, and disk space. Monitor system resources using the **top** or **htop** command:

```
top
```

If system resources are limited, consider optimizing Snort's configuration or running it on a more capable system.

Rule Loading Errors

Rule loading errors can occur if there are issues with Snort's rule files, such as syntax errors or missing rule sets.

To address this type of issue, review the rule files in the **/etc/snort/rules/** directory for syntax errors or incorrect rules. Use a text editor to make necessary corrections:

```
sudo nano /etc/snort/rules/local.rules
```

Run Snort in test mode to validate the rules and identify any errors:

```
sudo snort -T -c /etc/snort/snort.lua
```

If specific rule sets are missing, download and install them from reputable sources, such as the

Snort Community Rules or Emerging Threats.

Performance Issues

Snort may experience performance issues if the system is unable to handle high traffic volumes or if the configuration is not optimized. Now to overcome these performance issues, first verify that the system resources are sufficient to support Snort's operation. You can begin with monitoring or keeing a close eye to CPU, memory, and network usage using the **top** or **htop** command:

```
top
```

Then, optimize Snort's configuration by adjusting settings such as buffer sizes, timeout values, and preprocessor configurations. Edit the **snort.lua** file to make necessary changes.

Log File Issues

Log file issues can occur if Snort is unable to write to the specified log files or if the log files become too large. In this, verify the permissions of the log files and directories. Ensure that Snort has write access to the log directory:

```
ls -l /var/log/snort/
```

Rotate and manage log files to prevent them from becoming too large. Use log rotation tools, such as **logrotate**, to automatically manage log file sizes:

```
sudo apt install logrotate
```

Update Snort's configuration to specify appropriate log file paths and formats in the **snort.lua** file.

Kernel Module Conflicts

Kernel module conflicts can occur if there are compatibility issues between Snort and specific kernel modules or drivers.

Now here, check for kernel module conflicts using the **dmesg** command to review kernel logs:

```
dmesg | grep snort
```

Update the kernel and relevant drivers to the latest versions to resolve compatibility issues:

```
sudo apt update
```

```
sudo apt upgrade
```

You may consider using a different packet capture engine, such as AFPacket or netmap, if conflicts persist with the default packet capture engine.

Summary

In general, this chapter covered all the bases when it came to installing and configuring Snort 3. The chapter began by explaining how to use Snort's configuration files, specifically the snort.lua file, which allowed you to change network variables, preprocessors, rule paths, and output modules. The integration of tools such as Barnyard2 and BASE was highlighted, demonstrating how they improved Snort's functionality by efficiently processing logs and providing a user-friendly interface for monitoring alerts. In addition, part of this chapter focused on testing Snort's installation, which included running the program in IDS mode and simulating different attack scenarios to see how well it detected them. The chapter showed how to simulate common threats like port scans and ping flood attacks with tools like nmap and hping3. You also learned how to write custom rules to detect specific patterns in network traffic, ensuring that Snort performed well as a network security tool.

The chapter concluded with a thorough troubleshooting section that addressed potential problems encountered during installation and configuration. You were taught how to fix problems like missing dependencies, configuration errors, and network interface issues. Overall, this chapter provided you with the knowledge required to install, configure, and troubleshoot Snort 3, preparing you to use it as an essential component of your cybersecurity strategy.

CHAPTER 3: UP AND RUNNING WITH SNORT ARCHITECTURE AND OPERATIONS

Chapter Overview

This chapter provides an in-depth look at Snort's architecture and different ways of operation done through it. This chapter will look at Snort's core components, including the packet decoder, preprocessors, detection engine, and output modules. If you want to know how Snort processes network traffic to identify and react to threats, you should study how these parts work together. We will then look at the various modes in which Snort can be run, each with unique functionalities tailored to different network security scenarios. You'll learn how to use Snort's modes to meet your specific security requirements, including sniffer mode, which captures and displays packets in real time, and IDS mode, which actively monitors and analyzes traffic. The chapter will also go over the necessary command-line options and utilities that improve Snort's operations, allowing you to configure and manage Snort effectively from the command line.

Next, an essential part of using Snort is capturing and analyzing network traffic and here, you will learn how to effectively capture traffic and use Snort to detect suspicious activity. Furthermore, the chapter will go over Snort's performance tuning techniques, which will allow you to optimize Snort for high-performance environments and ensure it runs efficiently even under heavy network loads. Overall, this chapter will provide you with a thorough understanding of Snort's architecture and operations, allowing you to deploy and manage Snort as a powerful network security tool. With this knowledge, you'll be able to fully utilize Snort's capabilities, ensuring that your network is protected from evolving cyber threats.

Snort 3 Architecture

Snort 3 is a versatile and powerful intrusion detection and prevention system that leverages a modular architecture to provide comprehensive network security. This architecture allows Snort to be flexible, extensible, and highly efficient in detecting and responding to various cyber threats. Understanding Snort's architecture is essential for configuring and optimizing it to suit your specific security needs. In this section, we will explore the key components of Snort's modular architecture and the functions they perform.

Snort's architecture is designed around a modular framework that separates different aspects of its operation into distinct components. This separation allows each component to focus on a specific task, making Snort more adaptable to different network environments and security requirements. The main components of Snort's architecture include the packet decoder, preprocessors, detection engine, and output modules. Each component works together to analyze network traffic and generate alerts for potential threats.

Packet Decoder

The packet decoder is the first component in Snort's processing pipeline. It captures raw network packets from the specified network interface and translates them into a format that can be analyzed by Snort. The packet decoder performs several critical functions, including identifying the network protocol, extracting packet headers, and normalizing packet data for further analysis. By decoding packets into a standardized format, Snort can accurately process and inspect network traffic across various protocols.

The packet decoder supports a wide range of network protocols, including Ethernet, IP, TCP, UDP, and ICMP. It also handles non-IP protocols such as ARP and VLAN, ensuring comprehensive coverage of network traffic. The decoder's ability to process multiple protocol types enables Snort to monitor diverse network environments effectively. Additionally, the packet decoder can identify fragmented packets and reconstruct them for complete analysis, which is essential for detecting evasion techniques that rely on packet fragmentation.

Preprocessors

Preprocessors are modular components that extend Snort's capabilities by performing specific analysis tasks on network traffic before it reaches the detection engine. They play a crucial role in enhancing Snort's threat detection capabilities by normalizing traffic, detecting anomalies, and preparing packets for further inspection. Preprocessors can be customized and configured to address the unique needs of different network environments, allowing Snort to adapt to evolving threats and attack vectors.

Some of the key preprocessors in Snort 3 include:

Stream Preprocessor

The stream preprocessor is responsible for TCP stream reassembly, allowing Snort to analyze complete sessions rather than individual packets. This capability is essential for detecting multi-packet attacks and threats that occur across multiple segments of a TCP stream. By reassembling streams, Snort can accurately detect threats such as TCP-based buffer overflows and session hijacking attempts.

Frag3 Preprocessor

The frag3 preprocessor handles IP fragmentation, allowing Snort to reconstruct fragmented packets for comprehensive analysis. This preprocessor is critical for detecting attacks that use fragmentation to evade detection, such as fragmentation-based evasion techniques and overlapping fragment attacks. By reassembling fragmented packets, Snort can accurately identify and alert on these threats.

HTTP Inspect Preprocessor

The HTTP inspect preprocessor analyzes HTTP traffic to detect web-based threats, such as cross-site scripting (XSS), SQL injection, and directory traversal attacks. It inspects HTTP headers, payloads, and URLs for suspicious patterns and anomalies, enabling Snort to detect and respond to web application attacks effectively. This preprocessor is particularly valuable for protecting web servers and applications from common web-based threats.

SSL Preprocessor

The SSL preprocessor inspects encrypted SSL/TLS traffic, allowing Snort to detect threats that occur within encrypted sessions. It performs tasks such as decrypting SSL/TLS traffic, analyzing SSL handshake messages, and identifying suspicious SSL certificate anomalies. This preprocessor is essential for detecting attacks that use encryption to bypass traditional security measures, such as encrypted malware communications and SSL-based evasion techniques.

DNS Preprocessor

The DNS preprocessor analyzes DNS traffic to detect DNS-based attacks, such as DNS tunneling, cache poisoning, and DNS amplification attacks. It inspects DNS queries and responses for suspicious patterns and anomalies, enabling Snort to detect and respond to DNS-related threats effectively. This preprocessor is particularly valuable for protecting DNS infrastructure and ensuring the integrity of DNS services.

ARP Preprocessor

The ARP preprocessor analyzes ARP traffic to detect ARP-based attacks, such as ARP spoofing and ARP poisoning. It inspects ARP packets for anomalies and inconsistencies, enabling Snort to detect and respond to ARP-related threats effectively. This preprocessor is essential for protecting network infrastructure from ARP-based attacks that can compromise network security.

Other Preprocessors

Snort 3 supports a variety of additional preprocessors, each designed to address specific types of threats and network traffic. These preprocessors can be enabled or disabled based on the specific needs of your network environment, allowing you to tailor Snort's capabilities to suit your security requirements.

Detection Engine

The detection engine is the core component of Snort's architecture, responsible for evaluating network traffic against a set of predefined rules to identify potential threats. It uses a signature-based approach to detect known attack patterns and anomalies, allowing Snort to generate alerts for suspicious activities. The detection engine's ability to process and analyze large volumes of network traffic in real-time makes it a critical component of Snort's intrusion detection and prevention capabilities.

The detection engine supports various rule types, including:

Signature-Based Rules

Signature-based rules rely on predefined patterns or signatures to identify known threats. These rules specify conditions, such as specific payload patterns or header values, that must be met for an alert to be generated. Signature-based detection is effective for identifying well-known threats and attack vectors, such as malware signatures and vulnerability exploits.

Anomaly-Based Rules

Anomaly-based rules detect deviations from normal network behavior, allowing Snort to identify unknown or emerging threats. These rules define baselines for expected network activity and generate alerts when traffic deviates from these baselines. Anomaly-based detection is valuable for identifying zero-day attacks and advanced persistent threats (APTs) that may not have known signatures.

Behavior-Based Rules

Behavior-based rules focus on detecting suspicious behavior patterns rather than specific signatures. These rules analyze the behavior of network traffic and identify activities that may indicate malicious intent, such as unusual login attempts or data exfiltration patterns.

Behavior-based detection is effective for identifying insider threats and attacks that rely on social engineering.

Protocol-Specific Rules

Protocol-specific rules target specific network protocols, such as HTTP, DNS, or SMB, to detect protocol-specific threats and anomalies. These rules leverage Snort's preprocessors to analyze protocol-specific traffic and identify potential threats within the protocol context.

Protocol-specific detection is essential for protecting network services and applications from protocol-based attacks.

Output Modules

Output modules are responsible for handling Snort's alerts and logs, determining how and where the information is recorded or sent. These modules allow Snort to integrate with other security tools and systems, enabling centralized logging, alert management, and incident response. Output modules provide flexibility in how Snort's data is used and consumed, allowing organizations to tailor their security operations to their specific needs.

Some of the key output modules in Snort 3 include:

Unified2 Output

The unified2 output module is a binary logging format that captures Snort's alerts and logs for further analysis. It is designed for efficient storage and retrieval of Snort's data, allowing for easy integration with external analysis tools and systems, such as Security Information and Event Management (SIEM) platforms. The unified2 format is commonly used for high-performance environments where rapid data processing is essential.

Syslog Output

The syslog output module sends Snort's alerts and logs to the system's syslog service, enabling centralized logging and alert management. Syslog integration allows Snort to work seamlessly with existing logging infrastructure, providing a consistent and reliable method for capturing and analyzing security events. Syslog output is particularly valuable for organizations with established syslog-based monitoring and alerting systems.

Fast Alert Output

The fast alert output module generates human-readable alerts in a simplified format, allowing for quick and easy interpretation of Snort's detections. Fast alert output is useful for situations where rapid response to security events is required, such as in Security Operations Centers (SOCs) or incident response teams. The fast alert format provides a concise and actionable representation of Snort's detections.

Database Output

The database output module stores Snort's alerts and logs in a database, enabling advanced querying and analysis capabilities. This module allows organizations to build custom dashboards and reports, providing deeper insights into network security trends and threat patterns. Database output is ideal for organizations that require detailed historical analysis of security events.

Custom Output

Snort 3 supports custom output modules, allowing organizations to develop their own methods for handling alerts and logs. Custom output modules can be tailored to specific security requirements, enabling seamless integration with proprietary tools and systems. This flexibility allows organizations to leverage Snort's data in innovative ways, enhancing their overall security posture.

Modular Architecture Benefits

Snort's modular architecture offers several key benefits that enhance its effectiveness as an intrusion detection and prevention system:

- The modular design allows Snort to be easily customized and extended to meet the unique needs of different network environments. Organizations can enable or disable specific modules based on their security requirements, ensuring that Snort operates optimally for their specific use case.
- Snort's architecture is designed to handle high volumes of network traffic, making it

suitable for deployment in large-scale enterprise environments. The modular components can be distributed across multiple instances of Snort, allowing organizations to scale their security operations as needed.

- The modular framework enables the development of additional components and plugins, allowing Snort to adapt to emerging threats and attack vectors. Organizations can develop custom preprocessors, rules, and output modules to enhance Snort's capabilities and address new security challenges.

By separating different aspects of its operation into distinct modules, Snort can efficiently process and analyze network traffic in real-time. Each module focuses on a specific task, ensuring that Snort operates with high performance and minimal latency.

Running Snort in Different Modes

Snort 3 can operate in different modes to fulfill various network security needs. Each mode provides specific functionalities that cater to distinct aspects of traffic monitoring and analysis. Understanding these modes allows you to leverage Snort's capabilities effectively and tailor its operation to your particular security requirements. In this section, we will explore the three primary modes of Snort: Sniffer Mode, Packet Logger Mode, and Network Intrusion Detection Mode. We will learn what each mode does and how to run Snort in these modes to achieve the desired security outcomes.

Sniffer Mode

Sniffer Mode is the most basic operating mode of Snort, where it functions as a packet sniffer, capturing and displaying network packets in real-time. This mode is similar to tools like **`tcpdump`** and **`Wireshark`** in that it provides raw access to network traffic without performing any detection or logging. Sniffer Mode is useful for analyzing network behavior, troubleshooting connectivity issues, and gaining insights into the data traversing a network.

Functions of Sniffer Mode

In Sniffer Mode, Snort captures all network packets from the specified interface and outputs the data to the console in a human-readable format. This output includes information about the packet headers, such as source and destination IP addresses, port numbers, and protocol types. Additionally, the payload data of each packet is displayed, allowing you to check the contents of the network traffic.

Sniffer Mode is ideal for situations where you need to observe the flow of packets through a network in real-time. It enables you to monitor live traffic and understand the types of data being exchanged. While Sniffer Mode does not provide any detection or alerting capabilities, it serves as a valuable tool for gaining visibility into network activity and identifying patterns or anomalies that may require further investigation.

Running Snort in Sniffer Mode

To run Snort in Sniffer Mode, you must specify the network interface you want to monitor. This is done using the **-i** option, which tells Snort to capture packets from the specified interface. Additionally, the **-v** option enables verbose output, displaying packet details on the console.

Following is an example:

```
sudo snort -i eth0 -v
```

In the above code,

- -i eth0: Specifies the network interface to monitor (replace **eth0** with the appropriate interface name for your system).
- -v: Enables verbose output, displaying packet details on the console.

Running this command starts Snort in Sniffer Mode, capturing and displaying packets from the specified interface. You can observe the packets in real-time, analyzing the headers and payloads as they traverse the network.

Packet Logger Mode

Packet Logger Mode is another operational mode of Snort that focuses on capturing and logging network packets for later analysis. Unlike Sniffer Mode, which displays packets in real-time, Packet Logger Mode saves the captured packets to disk in a specified directory. This mode is useful for recording traffic over time, creating a record of network activity that can be reviewed and analyzed offline.

Functions of Packet Logger Mode

In Packet Logger Mode, Snort captures network packets from the specified interface and writes them to log files in the designated directory. These log files contain detailed information about each packet, including headers and payloads. Packet Logger Mode allows you to store traffic data for extended periods, making it possible to perform historical analysis, conduct forensic investigations, and identify trends or patterns in network behavior.

The log files created in Packet Logger Mode can be analyzed using various tools, such as **tcpdump**, **Wireshark**, or Snort itself. This capability is particularly valuable for security analysts who need to check the network traffic in detail, identify anomalies, or investigate security incidents that occurred in the past.

Running Snort in Packet Logger Mode

To run Snort in Packet Logger Mode, you need to specify the network interface to capture packets from and the directory where the log files will be stored. This is done using the **-i** option for the interface and the **-l** option for the log directory.

Following is an example:

```
sudo snort -i eth0 -l /var/log/snort/
```

In the above code,

- -i eth0: Specifies the network interface to monitor (replace **eth0** with the appropriate interface name for your system).
- -l /var/log/snort/: Specifies the directory where the log files will be stored.

Running this command starts Snort in Packet Logger Mode, capturing packets from the specified interface and writing them to log files in the designated directory. You can analyze these log files later to gain insights into network activity and investigate potential security issues.

Network Intrusion Detection Mode

Network Intrusion Detection Mode (NIDS Mode) is the most advanced and widely used mode of Snort. In this mode, Snort operates as a full-fledged IDS, analyzing network traffic in real-time and generating alerts for suspicious activities. NIDS Mode leverages Snort's detection engine and rule sets to identify potential threats and notify security personnel of security incidents.

Functions of Network Intrusion Detection Mode

In Network Intrusion Detection Mode, Snort examines network packets from the specified interface and compares them against a set of predefined detection rules. These rules define patterns or conditions that indicate potential threats, such as known attack signatures, suspicious payloads, or protocol anomalies. When a packet matches a rule, Snort generates an alert, providing details about the detected threat.

NIDS Mode allows Snort to monitor network traffic continuously, providing real-time visibility into security threats and incidents. It enables organizations to detect a wide range of threats, including malware, unauthorized access attempts, and denial-of-service attacks. By generating alerts, Snort informs security personnel of potential security issues, enabling them to respond promptly and mitigate risks.

Running Snort in Network Intrusion Detection Mode

To run Snort in Network Intrusion Detection Mode, you need to specify the network interface to monitor and the configuration file containing the detection rules. This is done using the **-i** option for the interface and the **-c** option for the configuration file.

Following is the sample command:

```
sudo snort -i eth0 -c /etc/snort/snort.lua
```

In the above code,

- -i eth0: Specifies the network interface to monitor (replace **eth0** with the appropriate interface name for your system).
- -c /etc/snort/snort.lua: Specifies the configuration file containing the detection rules and settings.

Running this command starts Snort in Network Intrusion Detection Mode, analyzing packets from the specified interface and generating alerts for detected threats. The alerts are typically logged to the **/var/log/snort/alert** file, providing a record of security incidents for review and analysis.

Snort Modes Use Cases

Each of Snort's modes can be applied to various practical use cases, depending on the specific needs of your network environment and security strategy:

Sniffer Mode Use Cases

- Use Sniffer Mode to monitor real-time network traffic and identify connectivity problems, packet loss, or configuration errors.
- Gain insights into the types of data being transmitted across the network and observe communication patterns between devices.
- Use Sniffer Mode as a learning tool to study network protocols and packet structures, gaining hands-on experience with live network traffic.

Packet Logger Mode Use Cases

- Capture and store network traffic for later analysis, allowing you to examine packet contents and identify trends or patterns in network behavior.
- Use Packet Logger Mode to create a historical record of network activity, enabling you to investigate security incidents and trace potential breaches.
- Maintain detailed logs of network traffic to meet compliance requirements and demonstrate adherence to security policies.

Network Intrusion Detection Mode Use Cases

- Monitor network traffic continuously, detecting and alerting on potential threats as they occur.
- Use NIDS Mode to identify and respond to security incidents promptly, mitigating risks

and minimizing the impact of attacks.

- Implement NIDS Mode as part of a comprehensive security strategy, providing ongoing visibility into network threats and vulnerabilities.

Each of the above modes serve a unique purpose, catering to distinct use cases and scenarios, making Snort a versatile and powerful tool in the cybersecurity landscape. As you explore these modes, you'll gain a deeper understanding of Snort's capabilities and how it can be leveraged to enhance your organization's security posture.

Command-Line Options and Utilities

Snort's command-line arguments provide a way to configure and control Snort's operations directly from the terminal. These arguments allow you to specify various parameters, such as configuration files, network interfaces, and logging options. Below, we explore some of the most commonly used command-line arguments and how to use them effectively.

Common Snort Command-Line Arguments

-i <interface>

The -i argument specifies the network interface that Snort will monitor. This argument is essential when running Snort in any mode, as it determines the source of the network traffic that Snort will analyze.

Following is the example:

```
sudo snort -i eth0
```

In the above, Snort is set to monitor the **eth0** network interface.

-c <config_file>

The **-c** argument specifies the configuration file that Snort will use. This file contains the settings, rules, and preprocessors that Snort will apply during operation. The configuration file is the backbone of Snort's functionality, as it defines how Snort processes network traffic.

Following is the example:

```
sudo snort -c /etc/snort/snort.lua
```

This command tells Snort to use the **/etc/snort/snort.lua** configuration file.

-T

The **-T** argument runs Snort in test mode, verifying the configuration file and rule set without starting packet capture. This mode is useful for checking the syntax and validity of your configuration and rules before deploying Snort in a live environment.

Following is the example:

```
sudo snort -T -c /etc/snort/snort.lua
```

This command tests the configuration file for errors without starting Snort in active monitoring mode.

-l <log_directory>

The **-l** argument specifies the directory where Snort will store its log files. This argument is useful when running Snort in Packet Logger Mode or Network Intrusion Detection Mode, as it determines the location of captured packet logs and alerts.

Following is the example:

```
sudo snort -l /var/log/snort/
```

In this, Snort logs data to the **/var/log/snort/** directory.

-v

The **-v** argument enables verbose output, displaying detailed information about captured packets on the console. This option is typically used in Sniffer Mode to provide real-time visibility into network traffic.

Following is the example:

```
sudo snort -v -i eth0
```

This command runs Snort in Sniffer Mode with verbose output enabled.

-A <alert_mode>

The **-A** argument sets the alert mode, determining how Snort generates and displays alerts. Various alert modes include **full**, **fast**, **none**, and **unsock**, each offering different levels of detail and output formats.

Following is the example:

```
sudo snort -A fast -i eth0 -c /etc/snort/snort.lua
```

This command runs Snort in Network Intrusion Detection Mode with fast alert output, providing concise alert messages.

-K <log_mode>

The **-K** argument sets the logging mode, specifying the format of log files generated by Snort. Common log modes include **ascii**, **pcap**, and **unified2**, each offering different formats for storing packet data.

Following is the example:

```
sudo snort -K ascii -l /var/log/snort/
```

This command logs packets in ASCII format, making them human-readable for easier analysis.

-q

The **-q** argument runs Snort in quiet mode, suppressing most output messages to the console. This option is useful for running Snort in the background or integrating it into automated scripts.

Following is the example:

```
sudo snort -q -i eth0 -c /etc/snort/snort.lua
```

This command runs Snort quietly, minimizing console output.

-d

The **-d** argument enables decoding of packet payloads, displaying application-layer data in verbose mode. This option is useful for examining packet contents in detail during Sniffer Mode.

Following is the example:

```
sudo snort -d -v -i eth0
```

This command captures and displays packet payloads in detail.

--daq <type>

The **--daq** argument specifies the Data Acquisition (DAQ) module that Snort will use for packet capture. DAQ modules provide different packet I/O methods, such as **pcap**, **afpacket**, and **netmap**.

Following is the example:

```
sudo snort --daq pcap -i eth0 -c /etc/snort/snort.lua
```

This command uses the **pcap** DAQ module for packet capture.

Popular Snort Utilities and Tools

In addition to its command-line arguments, Snort is supported by a variety of utilities and tools that enhance its functionality and provide additional capabilities. These utilities allow you to analyze Snort's output, manage rules, and integrate Snort with other security tools. Below, we explore some of the most popular Snort utilities and tools used by the Snort community.

Barnyard2

Barnyard2 is a popular tool that processes Snort's unified2 output files, converting them into different formats and sending them to various output destinations. Barnyard2 acts as an intermediary between Snort and external analysis tools, enabling efficient handling of Snort's alerts and logs.

Following are the key functions of Barnyard2:

- Barnyard2 can store Snort alerts and logs in a database, such as MySQL or PostgreSQL, enabling advanced querying and analysis capabilities.
- By offloading the processing of Snort's output to Barnyard2, you can reduce the load on Snort and improve its performance.
- Barnyard2 supports multiple output formats, allowing you to customize how Snort's data is stored and used.

Now, to run Barnyard2, you need to configure it with the appropriate options and output plugins. Below is an example command to run Barnyard2 with a MySQL database:

```
sudo barnyard2 -c /etc/snort/barnyard2.conf -d
/var/log/snort/ -f snort.log -w
/var/log/snort/barnyard2.waldo -q
```

In the above command,

- -c /etc/snort/barnyard2.conf: Specifies the configuration file for Barnyard2.
- -d /var/log/snort/: Specifies the directory where Snort's unified2 files are stored.
- -f snort.log: Specifies the base name of the unified2 files.
- -w /var/log/snort/barnyard2.waldo: Specifies the Waldo file for tracking

processed files.

- -q: Runs Barnyard2 quietly, minimizing console output.

PulledPork

PulledPork is a script used to automate the management and updating of Snort's rule sets. It simplifies the process of downloading, updating, and organizing Snort rules, ensuring that your Snort installation remains up-to-date with the latest threat signatures.

Following are the key functions of PulledPork:

- PulledPork automatically downloads and updates Snort rules from various sources, such as the Snort Community Rules and Emerging Threats.
- PulledPork organizes and categorizes rules, allowing you to enable or disable specific rules based on your security needs.
- PulledPork verifies rule compatibility with your Snort version, ensuring that your rule sets work correctly with your configuration.

To run PulledPork, you need to configure its **pulledpork.conf** file with the appropriate options and credentials for downloading rules. Below is an example command to run PulledPork:

```
sudo pulledpork.pl -c /etc/snort/pulledpork.conf -l
```

In the above sample command,

- -c /etc/snort/pulledpork.conf: Specifies the configuration file for PulledPork.
- -l: Enables the use of local rules.

SnortSnarf

SnortSnarf is a tool that generates HTML reports from Snort's log files, providing a user-friendly way to view and analyze Snort alerts. It organizes alerts into categories and presents them in an easy-to-read format, making it simpler to interpret Snort's detections.

Following are the functions of SnortSnarf:

- SnortSnarf processes Snort's log files and generates detailed HTML reports, allowing you to visualize and analyze alerts.
- SnortSnarf categorizes alerts based on their types, providing insights into the nature and severity of detected threats.
- SnortSnarf's HTML reports can be accessed through a web browser, providing a convenient interface for reviewing and sharing alert data.

Now, to run SnortSnarf, you need to provide it with the path to Snort's log files and the output directory for the HTML reports. Below is an example command to run SnortSnarf:

```
perl snortsnarf.pl -d /var/www/snortsnarf/
/var/log/snort/alert
```

Here in the above command,

- **-d /var/www/snortsnarf/**: Specifies the output directory for the HTML reports.
- **/var/log/snort/alert**: Specifies the path to Snort's alert log file.

BASE (Basic Analysis and Security Engine)

BASE is a web-based tool that provides a graphical interface for managing and analyzing Snort alerts. It offers advanced querying capabilities and customizable views, allowing you to gain deeper insights into Snort's detections.

Following are the functions of BASE:

- BASE allows you to view, categorize, and manage Snort alerts through a web interface, streamlining alert handling and analysis.
- BASE provides powerful search and filtering options, enabling you to query alerts based on various criteria, such as source IP, destination IP, and alert type.
- BASE supports customizable dashboards and views, allowing you to tailor the interface to your specific analysis needs.

Now, to set up and run BASE, you need a web server with PHP and a database to store Snort alerts. Below are the general steps to set up BASE:

- Install a web server with PHP support, such as Apache or Nginx.

```
sudo apt install apache2 php libapache2-mod-php
```

- Install a database server, such as MySQL or PostgreSQL, to store Snort alerts.

```
sudo apt install mysql-server
```

- Download BASE from its official website and extract it to the web server's document root.

```
wget
http://downloads.sourceforge.net/project/secureideas/base
/1.4.5/base-1.4.5.tar.gz
```

```
tar -xvzf base-1.4.5.tar.gz -C /var/www/html/
```

- Edit the BASE configuration file (**base_conf.php**) to specify database connection details and other settings.

```
sudo nano /var/www/html/base/base_conf.php
```

- Access BASE through a web browser by navigating to the web server's address (e.g., http://localhost/base).

BASE provides a user-friendly interface for managing and analyzing Snort alerts, making it a valuable tool for security analysts and incident responders.

With each of these command-line arguments, you can control Snort's operation and integrate it with other security tools seamlessly. Additionally, popular utilities like Barnyard2, PulledPork, SnortSnarf, and BASE enhance Snort's functionality, providing advanced analysis, reporting, and rule management capabilities.

Capturing and Analyzing Network Traffic

Capturing and analyzing network traffic is a core function of Snort 3, allowing it to identify potential threats and provide insights into network activity. In this section, we will explore how to capture traffic using Snort and analyze the captured packets to detect suspicious behavior. For consistency and gradual learning, we will use a sample project scenario involving a small corporate network. This project will be used throughout the book to illustrate various Snort functionalities and concepts.

In our sample project, we will simulate a small corporate network consisting of multiple devices, including web servers, databases, and client workstations. The GitforGits machine, set up in the virtual lab, will act as the central monitoring node, running Snort to capture and analyze network traffic. This setup provides a realistic environment to demonstrate how Snort can be used to monitor and protect a network from potential threats.

Capturing Traffic with Snort

Capturing network traffic involves setting up Snort to listen on a specified network interface and record the packets traversing the network. Snort can capture traffic in various modes, each serving different purposes. For this demonstration, we will run Snort in Packet Logger Mode to capture and store traffic data for subsequent analysis.

Setting up the Capture Environment

Before capturing traffic, ensure that your virtual lab is set up with the following components:

- GitforGits Machine: This virtual machine will run Snort to capture network traffic. Ensure that Snort and its dependencies are installed and configured.
- Node1 and Node2: These virtual machines will simulate client and server devices in the network, generating traffic for Snort to capture.
- Network Topology: The virtual lab is configured in a star topology with the GitforGits machine as the central node.

Capturing Traffic in Packet Logger Mode

To capture network traffic in Packet Logger Mode, follow these steps:

- Open a terminal on the GitforGits machine and run the following command to start Snort in Packet Logger Mode:

```
sudo snort -i eth0 -l /var/log/snort/ -K ascii
```

- Snort will now begin capturing network traffic on the specified interface, logging packets to the designated directory.

To generate traffic for Snort to capture, perform the following actions from Node1 and Node2:

- On Node1, run a ping test to the GitforGits machine to simulate ICMP traffic:

```
ping 192.168.56.101 -c 4
```

This command sends four ICMP echo requests to the GitforGits machine.

- On Node2, use **`curl`** to send an HTTP request to a web server running on the GitforGits machine (ensure a web server is running on the GitforGits machine):

```
curl http://192.168.56.101/index.html
```

This command sends an HTTP GET request to the GitforGits machine, simulating web traffic.

- After generating traffic, check the **`/var/log/snort/`** directory on the GitforGits machine to verify that packets have been captured:

```
ls /var/log/snort/
```

After all this, you should see log files in the directory, each containing captured packets from the network traffic.

Analyzing Captured Packets

Analyzing captured packets involves examining the contents of the log files generated by Snort to identify potential threats or anomalies. Snort's logs contain detailed information about each packet, including headers and payloads, which can be used to detect suspicious activities.

Tools for Packet Analysis

There are several tools available for analyzing captured packets, each offering different features and capabilities:

- Snort itself can be used to analyze captured packets, leveraging its rule sets and detection engine to identify threats.
- Wireshark is a popular network protocol analyzer that provides a graphical interface for examining packet details.
- tcpdump is a command-line tool for capturing and analyzing packets, providing a text-based alternative to Wireshark.

For the demonstrations, we will use Snort and Wireshark to analyze the captured packets.

Analyzing Packets with Snort

To analyze captured packets with Snort, you can run Snort in IDS Mode, specifying the log files as input:

- Open a terminal on the GitforGits machine and run the following command to analyze the captured packets:

```
sudo snort -r /var/log/snort/snort.log.<timestamp> -c
/etc/snort/snort.lua
```

In this, the Snort will process the captured packets, applying its detection rules to identify potential threats.

- After running Snort, review the alerts generated during the analysis. Alerts are typically logged to the **/var/log/snort/alert** file:

```
sudo cat /var/log/snort/alert
```

- And then assess the alert log for any suspicious activities or anomalies detected in the captured packets.

Analyzing Packets with Wireshark

Wireshark provides a graphical interface for analyzing captured packets, offering detailed insights into packet contents and network behavior.

- On the GitforGits machine, open Wireshark and select the log file to analyze:

```
wireshark /var/log/snort/snort.log.<timestamp>
```

- This above command launches Wireshark and loads the specified log file.
- Then, use Wireshark's interface to examine packet details, including headers and payloads. Use the Wireshark's filtering capabilities to view packets of specific protocols, such as ICMP or HTTP.

Identifying Suspicious Traffic Patterns

During packet analysis, certain traffic patterns and behaviors may indicate potential threats or security incidents. Below are some common signs of suspicious network activity to look for when analyzing captured packets:

Port Scanning

Port scanning is a technique used by attackers to identify open ports and services on a network. It involves sending packets to various ports and analyzing the responses to determine which ports are open.

Following are the symptoms of Port Scanning:

- A large number of packets sent to multiple ports in a short period.
- Repeated connection attempts to closed or filtered ports.

Snort can detect port scanning activities by identifying patterns consistent with scanning techniques, such as SYN scans or NULL scans. Look for alerts related to reconnaissance activities in the alert log.

Denial-of-Service (DoS) Attacks

DoS attacks aim to disrupt the availability of network services by overwhelming a target with excessive traffic. These attacks can consume bandwidth, resources, or connections, rendering the target inaccessible.

Following are the symptoms of DoS Attacks:

- A sudden increase in traffic volume, often from a single source or a few sources.
- Repeated requests or connections that saturate network resources.

Snort can detect DoS attacks by identifying traffic patterns consistent with attack techniques, such as SYN floods or ICMP floods. Review the alert log for indications of DoS activities.

Malware Communications

Malware often communicates with command-and-control (C2) servers to receive instructions or exfiltrate data. These communications may use specific protocols or payloads indicative of malicious behavior.

Following are the symptoms of Malware Communications:

- Unexpected outbound connections to unfamiliar or suspicious IP addresses.
- Traffic containing known malicious signatures or payloads.

Snort can detect malware communications by matching traffic against known signatures or identifying anomalies in protocol behavior. And then assess the alert log for signs of malicious communications.

Sample Program: Detecting an HTTP Attack

We will walk through a practical example of detecting an HTTP-based attack using Snort:

Simulate an HTTP Attack

On Node2, use **curl** to send a malicious HTTP request to the GitforGits machine, simulating an attack such as SQL injection:

```
curl "http://192.168.56.101/index.html?user=admin' OR
'1'='1"
```

This command sends an HTTP GET request with a payload indicative of SQL injection.

Analyze with Snort

Run Snort in IDS Mode on the GitforGits machine to analyze the captured packets:

```
sudo snort -r /var/log/snort/snort.log.<timestamp> -c
/etc/snort/snort.lua
```

Review Alerts

Check the alert log for any alerts related to the simulated HTTP attack:

```
sudo cat /var/log/snort/alert
```

Look for alerts indicating potential SQL injection or suspicious HTTP behavior.

Analyze with Wireshark

Open Wireshark and load the log file to examine packet details:

```
wireshark /var/log/snort/snort.log.<timestamp>
```

Use Wireshark's filters to identify the HTTP request and analyze its contents:

Then, filter it by HTTP protocol:

```
http
```

Then, assess the payload for signs of SQL injection or other malicious activity.

By leveraging Snort's Packet Logger Mode and integrating tools like Wireshark, you can effectively monitor, capture, and analyze packets to identify suspicious behavior. And through such practical examples, including simulating attacks and reviewing alerts, you learned hands-on experience in using Snort to protect your network from evolving cyber threats.

Snort Performance Tuning

When a network experiences a sudden spike in traffic, Snort may struggle to process all packets efficiently, leading to dropped packets, delayed alerts, or even system crashes. Effective performance tuning is essential to ensure that Snort operates optimally, even under heavy network loads. In this section, we will explore strategies for handling high traffic loads and enhancing Snort's performance to maintain reliable and efficient network security operations.

High Traffic Loads

High traffic loads occur when the volume of network packets exceeds Snort's processing capacity. This can happen during peak network usage, distributed denial-of-service (DDoS) attacks, or when a large number of devices are active on the network.

High traffic loads can lead to several issues, including:

- Snort may drop packets if it cannot process them quickly enough, potentially missing critical security events.
- High traffic loads can cause delays in packet processing, leading to slower detection and response times.
- Snort may consume excessive CPU, memory, and disk resources, impacting system performance and stability.

To address these challenges, it is important to implement performance tuning techniques that optimize Snort's operation and enhance its ability to handle high traffic loads.

Techniques for Handling High Traffic Loads

There are several strategies and techniques that can be employed to handle high traffic loads and improve Snort's performance. These strategies involve optimizing Snort's configuration, leveraging hardware resources, and using traffic management techniques.

Optimizing Snort Configuration

- Adjusting Preprocessor Settings

Preprocessors in Snort are responsible for tasks such as stream reassembly, traffic normalization, and anomaly detection. Tuning preprocessor settings can reduce overhead and improve performance.

The stream preprocessor handles TCP stream reassembly, which can be resource-intensive. You can adjust settings like max_sessions and timeout to optimize performance.

Following is the example:

```
stream = {

  max_sessions = 262144,

  timeout = 30,

}
```

In the above example,

  - max_sessions: Limits the maximum number of concurrent sessions. Increasing this value can improve performance under high traffic but may consume more memory.
  - timeout: Sets the timeout for inactive sessions. Reducing this value can free up resources for new sessions.

- Frag3 Preprocessor

The frag3 preprocessor handles IP fragmentation. You can adjust settings like **max_frags** and **timeout** to optimize performance. Following is the example:

```
frag3 = {
```

```
  max_frags = 4096,

  timeout = 60,

}
```

In the above example,

- max_frags: Limits the maximum number of fragments to track. Increasing this value can improve performance but may consume more memory.
- timeout: Sets the timeout for incomplete fragments. Reducing this value can free up resources for new fragments.

- Optimizing Detection Engine

The detection engine is responsible for evaluating packets against Snort's rule sets. Tuning the detection engine can enhance performance by reducing processing overhead. Also, Snort supports rule profiling, which provides insights into rule performance and resource usage. You can use rule profiling to identify and optimize resource-intensive rules. To do this, add the following option to the **snort.lua** configuration file:

```
detection = {

  enable_profiling = true,

}
```

In the above code, run Snort and review the profiling output to identify rules that consume the most resources. Then, you can then optimize or disable these rules to improve performance.

- Rule Ordering

Snort evaluates rules in the order they are loaded. Placing high-priority or frequently triggered rules at the top of the list can reduce processing time. We will take an example in which you place commonly triggered rules, such as port scans or known malware signatures, at the top of the rule set:

```
include $RULE_PATH/high_priority.rules

include $RULE_PATH/community.rules
```

- Packet Buffer

The packet buffer stores captured packets before processing. Increasing the buffer size can reduce packet loss during high traffic periods. Following is the example:

```
config = {
  packet_buffer_size = 32768,
}
```

In the above example, packet_buffer_size sets the size of the packet buffer in bytes. By increasing this value can improve performance but may consume more memory.

- Configuring Output Modules

Snort's output modules determine how alerts and logs are generated and stored. Optimizing output module settings can improve performance by reducing disk I/O. The unified2 output module provides efficient binary logging. Configuring unified2 settings can enhance performance.

Following is the example

```
output = {
  unified2 = {
    max_file_size = 104857600,
    log_path = "/var/log/snort/unified2",
  },
}
```

In this, max_file_size sets the maximum size of unified2 log files. By increasing this value can reduce disk I/O but may consume more disk space.

Leveraging Multi-Core Processing

Snort 3 supports multi-threading, allowing it to take advantage of multi-core processors for parallel packet processing. Enabling multi-threading can significantly improve performance under high traffic loads.

In this, to enable Multi-Threading, add the following option to the snort.lua configuration file:

```
config = {

  max_threads = 4,

}
```

The **max_threads** sets the number of threads for parallel processing. It adjusts this value based on the number of available CPU cores.

Sample Program: Enhancing Snort Performance

We will walk through a practical example of enhancing Snort's performance to handle high traffic loads effectively.

Suppose the corporate network is experiencing a distributed denial-of-service (DDoS) attack, causing a significant increase in traffic volume. The goal is to optimize Snort's performance to handle the high traffic load without dropping packets or missing alerts.

Optimize Preprocessor Settings

Adjust the stream and frag3 preprocessors to handle the increased number of sessions and fragments:

```
stream = {

  max_sessions = 524288,

  timeout = 20,

}


frag3 = {

  max_frags = 8192,

  timeout = 30,

}
```

Enable Multi-Threading

Configure Snort to use multiple threads for parallel processing:

```
config = {
  max_threads = 8,
}
```

This configuration leverages the multi-core capabilities of the server, improving packet processing speed.

Adjust Buffer Sizes

Increase the packet buffer size to reduce packet loss:

```
config = {
  packet_buffer_size = 65536,
}
```

Optimize Detection Engine

Enable rule profiling to identify and optimize resource-intensive rules:

```
detection = {
  enable_profiling = true,
}
```

Here,

- Review the profiling output and adjust rule ordering to prioritize high-frequency rules.
- Use VLANs and firewall rules to filter out irrelevant traffic, reducing the load on Snort.

Monitor Performance

Continuously monitor Snort's performance using system monitoring tools like **top** or **htop**:

```
htop
```

By running this, you can monitor CPU, memory, and network usage to ensure Snort operates efficiently.

These above performance tuning strategies ensure that Snort remains effective in detecting and responding to threats, even during peak network activity or DDoS attacks.

Summary

As a whole, our knowledge of Snort 3's architecture and operations allowed us to shed light on its modular design and various operating modes. It started by explaining Snort's modular architecture, focusing on key components like the packet decoder, preprocessors, detection engine, and output modules. These components worked together to effectively analyze network traffic and detect potential threats. The chapter then described how preprocessors prepared packets for analysis, the detection engine used rules to identify suspicious activity, and output modules controlled how alerts and logs were generated and stored.

The chapter then looked at Snort's various modes, including Sniffer Mode, Packet Logger Mode, and Network Intrusion Detection Mode (NIDS). Each mode served a specific purpose, ranging from simply capturing and displaying packets in Sniffer Mode to actively monitoring traffic and issuing alerts in NIDS Mode. By familiarizing themselves with these modes, you were able to adapt Snort's operations to your own needs and use it for a variety of network security missions. We also went over the command-line options and utilities of Snort, showing how various arguments could be used to change and manage how the program behaved. This included options for setting network interfaces, configuration files, and logging preferences. Not only that, but popular utilities like Barnyard2, PulledPork, SnortSnarf, and BASE were also introduced. These tools let you manage and analyze Snort data, update rules, and visualize alerts.

Finally, the chapter taught performance tuning, which included strategies for effectively managing high traffic loads. Techniques for improving Snort's performance and reliability included optimizing preprocessor settings, leveraging multi-core processing, and implementing traffic filtering.

Chapter 4: Writing Snort Rules

Chapter Overview

In order to adapt Snort's intrusion detection capabilities to your unique network security needs, this chapter will center on learning how to create and customize Snort rules. Snort rules define the patterns and behaviors that Snort looks for in network traffic, allowing it to detect and alert on potential threats more effectively. This chapter begins with an introduction to Snort rules' structure and syntax, providing the fundamental knowledge required to understand how rules are built and applied within Snort's detection engine.

Following the introduction, we will go over how to write basic Snort rules, which detect common network threats. This section dives into the essential components of a Snort rule, such as rule headers and options, and shows how to use them to detect various attack patterns. If you want to learn how to write more complicated rules for Snort, starting with the basics will give you the practical experience you need to tailor it to react to particular threats. We then move on to more advanced rule options and keywords, learning how to use them to create detailed and nuanced detection rules. Additional keywords that improve rule functionality, such as metadata, flow options, and content matching, are introduced in this section of the chapter. These advanced techniques enable you to fine-tune your rules, ensuring they are precise and efficient in detecting complex threats.

Finally, we learned to testing and debugging Snort rules, emphasizing the importance of validating rules in a controlled environment before deploying them in production. You'll learn how to evaluate rule effectiveness and troubleshoot problems to ensure peak performance. This comprehensive Snort rule writing approach provides you with the skills you need to improve the security posture of your network.

Introduction to Snort Rules

Concept of Snort Rules

Snort rules are essentially scripts that dictate how Snort analyzes network traffic and what actions it takes when a pattern of interest is detected. These rules allow Snort to perform deep packet inspection, examining the contents of each packet for known attack patterns or anomalies. Each rule consists of conditions and actions, specifying what Snort should look for and how it should respond when those conditions are met.

Snort rules play a crucial role in the effectiveness of an IDS. By writing specific rules, you can detect a wide range of attacks, from simple port scans to complex buffer overflow exploits. This customization capability makes Snort highly adaptable and capable of addressing various security challenges across different network environments.

Snort Rule: Syntax and Structure

Understanding the syntax and structure of Snort rules is essential for writing effective detection scripts. A Snort rule is composed of two main parts: the rule header and the rule options. Together, these components define the conditions that trigger an alert and the specific actions that Snort takes in response.

Rule Header

The rule header specifies the basic characteristics of the traffic that the rule applies to. It includes the action, protocol, source and destination IP addresses, and source and destination ports.

Given below is a breakdown of the components of a rule header:

- Action:
    - The action defines what Snort should do when a rule is triggered. Common actions include:
    - **alert**: Generates an alert when the rule conditions are met.
    - **log**: Logs the packet without generating an alert.
    - **pass**: Ignores the packet and continues processing.
    - **drop**: Drops the packet and logs the event (requires Snort to be in inline mode).
    - **reject**: Drops the packet and sends a TCP reset or ICMP unreachable message to the sender.
    - **sdrop**: Silently drops the packet without logging (requires Snort to be in inline mode).
- Protocol:
    - The protocol specifies the type of traffic the rule applies to, such as **tcp**, **udp**, **icmp**, or **ip**.
- Source IP Address
    - The source IP address indicates the origin of the traffic. It can be specified as a single IP, a CIDR block, or a variable (e.g., **$HOME_NET**).
- Source Port
    - The source port indicates the port from which the traffic originates. It can be a specific port, a range of ports, or any port (**any**).
- Direction Operator

    - The direction operator specifies the flow of traffic. It can be **->** (unidirectional) or **<>** (bidirectional).
- Destination IP Address
    - The destination IP address indicates the target of the traffic. Like the source IP, it can be specified as a single IP, a CIDR block, or a variable.
- Destination Port

  The destination port indicates the port to which the traffic is directed. It can be a specific port, a range of ports, or any port.

Following is an example of Rule Header:

```
alert tcp $EXTERNAL_NET any -> $HOME_NET 80
```

This above header indicates that the rule will generate an alert for TCP traffic from any external source (**$EXTERNAL_NET**) to port 80 on the home network (**$HOME_NET**).

Rule Options

Rule options provide additional criteria and metadata for the rule. They are enclosed in parentheses and separated by semicolons. Rule options include content matching, metadata, and other parameters that refine the rule's functionality.

- **Content**

The **content** option specifies a pattern to search for within the packet payload. It is one of the most powerful features of Snort rules, enabling deep packet inspection.

Following is the example:

```
content:"GET /index.html";
```

This option searches for the string "GET /index.html" in the packet payload.

- **Msg**

The **msg** option provides a text message that describes the alert. It is used for logging and reporting purposes.

Following is the example:

```
msg:"HTTP GET Request Detected";
```

- **Sid**

The **sid** (signature ID) option assigns a unique identifier to the rule. It is used to differentiate between rules and manage them effectively.

Following is the example:

```
sid:1000001;
```

- **Rev**

The **rev** (revision) option specifies the version of the rule. It is used to track changes and updates to rules.

Following is the example:

```
rev:1;
```

- **Classtype**

The **classtype** option assigns a classification to the rule, indicating the type or severity of the alert. Classtypes are defined in the **classification.config** file.

Following is the example:

```
classtype:web-activity;
```

- **Flow**

The **flow** option specifies the direction and state of traffic, such as **established**, **to_client**, or **to_server**.

Following is the example:

```
flow:to_server,established;
```

See the following is an example of a complex rule:

```
alert tcp $EXTERNAL_NET any -> $HOME_NET 80 (msg:"HTTP
GET Request Detected"; content:"GET /index.html";
flow:to_server,established; classtype:web-activity;
sid:1000001; rev:1;)
```

This rule generates an alert for TCP traffic from any external source to port 80 on the home network, specifically when a GET request for "/index.html" is detected.

Types of Snort Rules

Snort supports various types of rules, each serving different purposes and addressing specific security needs. Understanding these types of rules allows you to write effective rules tailored to your network's security requirements.

Signature-Based Rules

Signature-based rules rely on predefined patterns or signatures to detect known threats. These rules specify conditions, such as specific payload patterns or header values, that must be met for an alert to be generated. Signature-based detection is effective for identifying well-known threats and attack vectors, such as malware signatures and vulnerability exploits.

Following is the example:

```
alert tcp any any -> any 445 (msg:"SMB Exploit Detected";
content:"|eb 15 5b 31 c0 88 43 31|"; sid:1000002; rev:1;)
```

This rule detects a specific SMB exploit signature.

Protocol-Based Rules

Protocol-based rules target specific network protocols, such as HTTP, DNS, or SMTP, to detect protocol-specific threats and anomalies. These rules leverage Snort's preprocessors to analyze protocol-specific traffic and identify potential threats within the protocol context.

Following is the example:

```
alert http $EXTERNAL_NET any -> $HOME_NET 80 (msg:"HTTP
SQL Injection Attempt"; content:"' OR '1'='1"; nocase;
sid:1000003; rev:1;)
```

This above rule detects SQL injection attempts in HTTP traffic by searching for common SQL injection patterns.

Anomaly-Based Rules

Anomaly-based rules detect deviations from normal network behavior, allowing Snort to identify unknown or emerging threats. These rules define baselines for expected network activity and generate alerts when traffic deviates from these baselines. Anomaly-based detection is valuable for identifying zero-day attacks and advanced persistent threats (APTs) that may not have known signatures.

Following is the example:

```
alert icmp any any -> $HOME_NET any (msg:"ICMP Packet
Size Anomaly"; dsize:>1000; sid:1000004; rev:1;)
```

This rule generates an alert for ICMP packets with unusually large sizes, indicating a potential anomaly.

Behavior-Based Rules

Behavior-based rules focus on detecting suspicious behavior patterns rather than specific signatures. These rules analyze the behavior of network traffic and identify activities that may indicate malicious intent, such as unusual login attempts or data exfiltration patterns. Behavior-based detection is effective for identifying insider threats and attacks that rely on social engineering.

Following is the example:

```
alert tcp $HOME_NET any -> $EXTERNAL_NET 21 (msg:"FTP
Brute Force Attempt"; flow:to_server,established;
threshold:type threshold, track by_src, count 5, seconds
60; sid:1000005; rev:1;)
```

This rule detects brute force attempts on FTP servers by monitoring repeated login attempts within a short period.

Writing Snort Rules

We will walk through the process of writing a Snort rule to detect a specific type of network threat, such as a malicious file download via HTTP.

Suppose you want to detect attempts to download a malicious file named "malware.exe" from a web server. The goal is to create a Snort rule that generates an alert whenever this file is requested over HTTP.

Define the Rule Header

Determine the characteristics of the traffic to be monitored. In this case, we are interested in HTTP traffic from any external source to our web server:

```
alert tcp $EXTERNAL_NET any -> $HOME_NET 80
```

Add Rule Options

Specify the content to search for within the packet payload, along with other relevant options:

- Content Option: Search for the filename "malware.exe" in the HTTP request:

```
content:"GET /malware.exe";
```

- Message Option: Provide a descriptive message for the alert:

```
msg:"Malicious File Download Detected";
```

- Flow Option: Specify that the traffic is directed to the server and is part of an established connection:

```
flow:to_server,established;
```

- SID and Revision Options: Assign a unique signature ID and revision number to the rule:

```
sid:1000006; rev:1;
```

Complete the Rule

Combine the header and options to form the complete Snort rule:

```
alert tcp $EXTERNAL_NET any -> $HOME_NET 80
(msg:"Malicious File Download Detected"; content:"GET
/malware.exe"; flow:to_server,established; sid:1000006;
rev:1;)
```

This rule generates an alert whenever an HTTP GET request for "malware.exe" is detected, allowing you to identify and respond to potential malicious file downloads.

You can tailor Snort to your unique security requirements and improve its capability to identify various network threats by examining the various rule types and mastering the art of rule crafting.

Crafting Basic Snort Rules

Crafting Snort rules allows you to customize Snort's detection capabilities to meet your specific security needs. By writing rules, you define the patterns and behaviors that Snort should monitor in network traffic, enabling it to detect and respond to potential threats effectively. In this section, we will demonstrate how to write basic Snort rules for traffic detection and explore the use of rule headers and options to refine your detection criteria.

We will start by writing a few simple rules to detect different types of network traffic.

Detecting ICMP Echo Requests

ICMP echo requests are commonly used for network diagnostics and reachability tests. Detecting these packets can help identify potential reconnaissance activities, such as network mapping or host discovery.

Define the Rule Header

Specify the action, protocol, source and destination IP addresses, and ports. For ICMP echo requests, we are interested in ICMP traffic from any source to any destination:

```
alert icmp any any -> any any
```

Add Rule Options

Include options that specify the ICMP type and a descriptive message for the alert:

- ICMP Type Option: Match ICMP echo requests (type 8):

```
icmp_type:8;
```

- Message Option: Provide a message to describe the alert:

```
msg:"ICMP Echo Request Detected";
```

- SID and Revision Options: Assign a unique signature ID and revision number to the rule:

```
sid:1000007; rev:1;
```

Complete the Rule

Combine the header and options to form the complete Snort rule:

```
alert icmp any any -> any any (msg:"ICMP Echo Request
Detected"; icmp_type:8; sid:1000007; rev:1;)
```

This above rule generates an alert whenever an ICMP echo request (ping request) is detected, allowing you to monitor for potential reconnaissance activities.

Detecting HTTP Traffic

HTTP traffic is a common vector for attacks, including SQL injection, cross-site scripting (XSS), and malicious file downloads. Detecting HTTP requests can help identify potential web-based threats.

Define the Rule Header

Specify the action, protocol, source and destination IP addresses, and ports. For HTTP traffic, we are interested in TCP traffic from any source to port 80 on the home network:

```
alert tcp any any -> $HOME_NET 80
```

Add Rule Options

Include options that specify the content to match and a descriptive message for the alert:

- Content Option: Match HTTP requests containing the "User-Agent" header:

```
content:"User-Agent";
```

- Message Option: Provide a message to describe the alert:

```
msg:"HTTP Traffic Detected";
```

- SID and Revision Options: Assign a unique signature ID and revision number to the rule:

```
sid:1000008; rev:1;
```

Complete the Rule

Combine the header and options to form the complete Snort rule:

```
alert tcp any any -> $HOME_NET 80 (msg:"HTTP Traffic
Detected"; content:"User-Agent"; sid:1000008; rev:1;)
```

This above rule generates an alert whenever HTTP traffic containing the "User-Agent" header is detected, allowing you to monitor for potential web-based threats.

Detecting SSH Login Attempts

SSH is a widely used protocol for secure remote access, but it can also be a target for brute force attacks. Detecting SSH login attempts can help identify unauthorized access attempts.

Define the Rule Header

Specify the action, protocol, source and destination IP addresses, and ports. For SSH traffic, we are interested in TCP traffic from any source to port 22 on the home network:

```
alert tcp any any -> $HOME_NET 22
```

Add Rule Options

Include options that specify the content to match and a descriptive message for the alert:

- Content Option: Match SSH login attempts by searching for the "SSH-2.0" banner:

```
content:"SSH-2.0";
```

- Message Option: Provide a message to describe the alert:

```
msg:"SSH Login Attempt Detected";
```

- SID and Revision Options: Assign a unique signature ID and revision number to the rule:

```
sid:1000009; rev:1;
```

Complete the Rule

Combine the header and options to form the complete Snort rule:

```
alert tcp any any -> $HOME_NET 22 (msg:"SSH Login Attempt
Detected"; content:"SSH-2.0"; sid:1000009; rev:1;)
```

This rule generates an alert whenever an SSH login attempt is detected, allowing you to monitor for unauthorized access attempts.

Sample Program: Writing a Rule to Detect SQL Injection

We will walk through a practical example of writing a Snort rule to detect a potential SQL injection attempt in HTTP traffic. Suppose you want to detect SQL injection attempts targeting your web server. The goal is to create a Snort rule that generates an alert whenever suspicious SQL patterns are detected in HTTP requests.

In this, first specify the action, protocol, source and destination IP addresses, and ports. For SQL injection detection, we are interested in TCP traffic from any source to port 80 on the home network:

```
alert tcp $EXTERNAL_NET any -> $HOME_NET 80
```

Then, specify the content to match, along with other relevant options:

```
content:"' OR '1'='1";

msg:"SQL Injection Attempt Detected";

flow:to_server,established;

sid:1000011; rev:1;
```

Now, combine the header and options to form the complete Snort rule:

```
alert tcp $EXTERNAL_NET any -> $HOME_NET 80 (msg:"SQL
Injection Attempt Detected"; content:"' OR '1'='1";
nocase; flow:to_server,established; sid:1000011; rev:1;)
```

This rule generates an alert whenever an HTTP request containing a common SQL injection pattern is detected, allowing you to monitor for potential SQL injection attempts targeting your web server.

Advanced Rule Options and Keywords

Advanced rule options like content matching, pattern matching, flow analysis, byte tests, and PCRE (Perl Compatible Regular Expressions) enable more precise and nuanced threat detection, and each of these options allow Snort to perform deep packet inspection and identify complex attack patterns that might otherwise go unnoticed.

Content Matching

Content matching is a fundamental feature of Snort rules that involves searching for specific strings within the packet payload. This option is often used to identify known attack signatures or protocol anomalies.

Consider the following content matching example:

In this, we will create a rule to detect HTTP requests for the **/admin** page, which may indicate attempts to access restricted areas of a web server.

First, specify the action, protocol, source and destination IP addresses, and ports. For this example, we monitor HTTP traffic:

```
alert tcp $EXTERNAL_NET any -> $HOME_NET 80
```

Use the **content** keyword to search for the specific string **/admin** in the HTTP request:

```
content:"/admin";
```

Then, combine the header and content option:

```
alert tcp $EXTERNAL_NET any -> $HOME_NET 80 (msg:"Attempt
to Access Admin Page Detected"; content:"/admin";
sid:1000012; rev:1;)
```

This rule generates an alert when a request for the **/admin** page is detected, which might indicate an attempt to access administrative pages.

Pattern Matching with PCRE

PCRE allows you to use regular expressions to perform complex pattern matching within packet payloads. This option provides greater flexibility and precision in identifying specific attack patterns.

For example, we will create a rule to detect HTTP requests that include SQL injection attempts using the PCRE option.

First, specify the action, protocol, source and destination IP addresses, and ports:

```
alert tcp $EXTERNAL_NET any -> $HOME_NET 80
```

Use the **pcre** keyword to match SQL injection patterns with a regular expression:

```
pcre:"/(\%27)|(\')|(\-\-)|(\%23)|(#)/i";
```

This regular expression matches various SQL injection techniques, including single quotes and comments.

Combine the header and PCRE option:

```
alert tcp $EXTERNAL_NET any -> $HOME_NET 80 (msg:"SQL
Injection Attempt Detected"; pcre:"/(\%27)|(\')|(\-\-
)|(\%23)|(#)/i"; sid:1000013; rev:1;)
```

This rule generates an alert when a SQL injection pattern is detected in HTTP traffic, enabling the identification of SQL injection attempts.

Flow and Byte Test Options

In addition to content matching and pattern matching, Snort provides several advanced options for performing flow analysis and evaluating specific byte values within packets. These options enable Snort to detect more sophisticated threats by analyzing the context and characteristics of network traffic.

Flow Options

Flow options specify the direction and state of network traffic, allowing Snort to focus on specific flows or sessions. They are particularly useful for detecting threats based on traffic patterns and session states.

We will create a rule to detect FTP data transfers by monitoring the flow of traffic to the server.

Specify the action, protocol, source and destination IP addresses, and ports:

```
alert tcp $HOME_NET any -> $EXTERNAL_NET 21
```

Use the **flow** keyword to specify that the rule applies to established connections directed to the server:

```
flow:to_server,established;
```

Use the **content** keyword to match the FTP **RETR** command, indicating a data transfer:

```
content:"RETR";
```

Combine the header, flow, and content options:

```
alert tcp $HOME_NET any -> $EXTERNAL_NET 21 (msg:"FTP
Data Transfer Detected"; flow:to_server,established;
content:"RETR"; sid:1000014; rev:1;)
```

This rule generates an alert for FTP data transfers by detecting the **RETR** command in established connections to the server.

Byte Test Options

Byte test options allow Snort to evaluate specific byte values within packet payloads or headers. These options are useful for detecting threats based on precise byte-level patterns.

We will create a rule to detect DNS responses with a specific record type, such as an MX (Mail Exchange) record.

Specify the action, protocol, source and destination IP addresses, and ports:

```
alert udp $EXTERNAL_NET 53 -> $HOME_NET any
```

Use the **byte_test** keyword to evaluate the record type in the DNS response:

```
byte_test:1,=,15,0;
```

This option checks if the record type is equal to 15 (MX record) at byte position 0.

Combine the header and byte test option:

```
alert udp $EXTERNAL_NET 53 -> $HOME_NET any (msg:"DNS MX
Record Response Detected"; byte_test:1,=,15,0;
sid:1000015; rev:1;)
```

This rule generates an alert when a DNS response contains an MX record, which may be useful for identifying mail server queries.

Sample Program: Detecting Buffer Overflow Attempts

Suppose you want to detect buffer overflow attempts targeting a web server. The goal is to create a Snort rule that generates an alert when unusually large requests are detected.

As usual, specify the action, protocol, source and destination IP addresses, and ports:

```
alert tcp $EXTERNAL_NET any -> $HOME_NET 80
```

Match HTTP requests that include a **GET** method:

```
content:"GET";
```

Use the **byte_test** keyword to check if the payload size exceeds a certain threshold, indicating a potential buffer overflow:

```
byte_test:5,>,1000,0;
```

This option checks if the payload size is greater than 1000 bytes at byte position 0.

Combine the header, content, and byte test options:

```
alert tcp $EXTERNAL_NET any -> $HOME_NET 80
```

```
(msg:"Potential Buffer Overflow Attempt Detected";
content:"GET"; byte_test:5,>,1000,0; sid:1000016; rev:1;)
```

This rule generates an alert for HTTP requests with payloads exceeding 1000 bytes, indicating a potential buffer overflow attempt targeting the web server. Utilizing these content matching, pattern matching with PCRE, flow analysis, and byte tests, you can craft Snort rules that detect complex threats and provide enhanced security for your network.

Testing and Debugging Snort Rules

Before deploying Snort rules in a production environment, it's essential to test them in a controlled setting to ensure they trigger correctly and generate the expected alerts. Following is how to run custom Snort rules:

Running Custom Snort Rules

First, create a separate rule file for your custom rules. This helps organize and manage your rules effectively.

```
sudo nano /etc/snort/rules/custom.rules
```

Add your custom rules to this file. For example, a rule to detect a specific HTTP request pattern:

```
alert tcp $EXTERNAL_NET any -> $HOME_NET 80 (msg:"Custom
Rule: Suspicious HTTP Request Detected";
content:"/suspicious"; sid:2000001; rev:1;)
```

Modify the Snort configuration file (**`snort.lua`**) to include your custom rule file:

```
include "/etc/snort/rules/custom.rules"
```

Execute Snort with the configuration file that includes your custom rules:

```
sudo snort -c /etc/snort/snort.lua -i eth0
```

Now, generate network traffic that should trigger your custom rule. For example, use **`curl`** to send an HTTP request matching the rule pattern:

```
curl http://192.168.56.101/suspicious
```

This command sends an HTTP request to the server with the specified path, which should trigger the rule.

Debugging Snort Rules

Despite careful rule writing, issues may arise that prevent rules from triggering as expected. Debugging Snort rules involves identifying and resolving these issues to ensure accurate detection. Following are common situations and strategies for debugging Snort rules:

Situation 1: Rule Does Not Trigger

If a rule does not trigger when expected, there may be an issue with the rule syntax or the traffic pattern not matching the rule criteria.

Now to debug this, firstly double-check the syntax of the rule to ensure there are no errors. Ensure all parentheses and semicolons are correctly placed.

```
alert tcp $EXTERNAL_NET any -> $HOME_NET 80
(msg:"Suspicious HTTP Request Detected";
content:"/suspicious"; sid:2000001; rev:1;)
```

Ensure the test traffic you generated matches the rule criteria. Use packet capture tools like **tcpdump** to analyze the traffic:

```
sudo tcpdump -i eth0 -A -s 0 port 80
```

Verify that the traffic contains the expected patterns, such as **/suspicious** in the HTTP request.

Then, run Snort in verbose mode to get more detailed output and understand how traffic is being processed:

```
sudo snort -c /etc/snort/snort.lua -i eth0 -v
```

Observe the output to identify any issues with rule matching.

Situation 2: Rule Triggers Unintentionally

A rule may trigger for unexpected traffic, leading to false positives. This can occur if the rule is too broad or lacks specificity. To resolve this issue, first ensure the **content** option is specific enough to avoid unintended matches. Add additional keywords or context to narrow the search:

```
content:"GET /suspicious"; http_method;
```

You may also use **flow** options to specify the direction and state of traffic, reducing false positives by focusing on relevant sessions:

```
flow:to_server,established;
```

Try consider adding additional options like **dsize** or **flags** to further refine the rule:

```
dsize:>100;

flags:A+;
```

These options can help eliminate irrelevant traffic and focus on specific conditions.

Situation 3: Performance Issues

Complex or inefficient rules can impact Snort's performance, leading to dropped packets or delayed alerts.

In this, first enable rule profiling to identify resource-intensive rules:

```
detection = {

  enable_profiling = true,

}
```

Then, review the profiling output to identify rules that consume the most resources and optimize them accordingly. Try to place high-priority or frequently triggered rules at the top of the rule set to reduce processing time:

```
include $RULE_PATH/high_priority.rules

include $RULE_PATH/custom.rules
```

If using PCRE, ensure that regular expressions are efficient and not overly complex.

Sample Program: Debugging Rule for Malicious File Downloads

We will walk through a practical example of debugging and optimizing a Snort rule to detect HTTP requests for potentially malicious files. Suppose you have a rule to detect downloads of a file named **malware.exe** but notice that it is not triggering correctly.

```
alert tcp $EXTERNAL_NET any -> $HOME_NET 80
(msg:"Malicious File Download Detected";
content:"/malware.exe"; sid:2000004; rev:1;)
```

Ensure the rule syntax is correct, and no characters are missing. Once this is done, use **tcpdump** to capture and analyze traffic:

```
sudo tcpdump -i eth0 -A -s 0 port 80
```

Check if the traffic contains the expected URL path **/malware.exe**. After this, run Snort in verbose mode to observe traffic processing:

```
sudo snort -c /etc/snort/snort.lua -i eth0 -v
```

Verify that the packet matches the rule criteria. Once done, add HTTP method and flow options to refine detection:

```
alert tcp $EXTERNAL_NET any -> $HOME_NET 80
(msg:"Malicious File Download Detected"; content:"GET
/malware.exe"; http_method; flow:to_server,established;
sid:2000004; rev:2;)
```

Then, add metadata for categorization:

```
metadata:service http, policy security-ips;
```

If using PCRE, ensure efficiency:

```
pcre:"/malware\.exe/i";
```

These above steps ensure that your Snort rules are accurate, efficient, and capable of detecting the intended threats without unnecessary overhead or false positives.

Summary

Generally speaking, this chapter trained us on how to write Snort rules that improve Snort's intrusion detection capabilities. It began by explaining the syntax and structure of Snort rules, which include a rule header and rule options. The rule header defines the basic characteristics of the traffic being monitored, such as the action, protocol, source and destination IP addresses, and ports. The chapter then demonstrated how to write basic Snort rules, guiding learners through the process of detecting common network threats like ICMP echo requests, HTTP traffic, and SSH login attempts. Advanced rule options and keywords were also learnt, including content matching, pattern matching with PCRE, flow analysis, and byte tests. These advanced options enabled Snort to perform deep packet inspection and identify sophisticated attack patterns, resulting in more precise and nuanced detection of complex threats.

Finally, the chapter talked about testing and debugging Snort rules, emphasizing the importance of validating rule functionality and optimizing performance. Learners were taught how to run custom rules, debug problems like unintentional triggers or performance bottlenecks, and optimize rules for efficiency. We spoke about ways to improve rule management and effectiveness by using variables, merging related rules, and utilizing metadata. Overall, this chapter gave us a thorough understanding of writing, testing, and optimizing Snort rules.

CHAPTER 5: WORKING WITH PREPROCESSORS AND EVENT PROCESSING

Chapter Overview

This chapter will look at Snort preprocessors and event processing, both of which are critical components for improving Snort's detection and analysis capabilities. In order to get network traffic ready for analysis, preprocessors normalize data and look for abnormalities before it reaches Snort's detection engine. This chapter begins with a study of Snort preprocessors, providing information about their functions and how they contribute to increased threat detection accuracy and efficiency.

We will then look at how to configure and tune preprocessors for optimal performance in specific network environments. This section will walk you through the configuration options available for various preprocessors and explain how to customize settings to meet your security needs. By learning how to effectively configure and tune preprocessors, you can improve Snort's ability to detect threats and reduce false positives. The chapter also teaches advanced preprocessor usage, emphasizing methods for using preprocessors to handle complex traffic scenarios and detect sophisticated threats. You'll learn how advanced preprocessor features can be used to improve Snort's detection capabilities and address specific security issues.

Finally, we will look at event processing and output plugins, which are essential for managing Snort alerts and logs. This section will walk you through the different output plugins available in Snort and show you how to configure them to handle alert data efficiently. You will learn how to effectively manage alerts and logs, so that Snort's output is both actionable and understandable. This chapter will teach you all you need to know to get the most out of Snort's event processing and preprocessing features for secure networks.

Understanding Snort Preprocessors

What are Preprocessors?

In Snort, preprocessors are modular components that operate on network traffic before it reaches the detection engine. They perform various preprocessing tasks such as packet normalization, fragmentation reassembly, and anomaly detection. Preprocessors act as intermediaries between the raw packet capture and the rule-based detection engine, enabling Snort to process traffic more effectively and accurately.

Preprocessors serve several key purposes:

- Preprocessors normalize network traffic to ensure consistent data representation. This involves transforming packets into a standardized format that the detection engine can analyze efficiently.
- Preprocessors analyze specific protocols, such as HTTP, DNS, or SMTP, to detect protocol-specific anomalies and threats. This analysis helps identify suspicious behaviors or patterns that might indicate an attack.

- Preprocessors detect anomalies in network traffic, such as unusual packet sizes or unexpected protocol behaviors. This capability allows Snort to identify potential threats that may not have known signatures.
- Preprocessors handle packet fragmentation and TCP stream reassembly, allowing Snort to analyze complete sessions rather than individual packets. This is crucial for detecting multi-packet attacks that span multiple segments.

Functionalities of Preprocessors

Preprocessors perform a wide range of functionalities that enhance Snort's ability to detect and respond to threats. Given below are some of the key functionalities provided by Snort preprocessors:

Packet Normalization

Packet normalization involves modifying packets to ensure consistent data representation, which helps the detection engine accurately analyze traffic. This process includes tasks such as adjusting TTL values, removing padding, and reordering TCP options. Packet normalization prevents evasion techniques that rely on packet manipulation to bypass IDSs.

For example, the Frag3 preprocessor is responsible for normalizing fragmented IP packets and reassembling them into complete datagrams for analysis. It identifies and reconstructs fragmented packets, ensuring they are processed correctly by the detection engine.

Protocol Decoding

Protocol decoding preprocessors analyze specific protocols to detect anomalies and potential threats within protocol-specific traffic. These preprocessors inspect protocol headers and payloads, identifying patterns or behaviors that may indicate malicious activity.

For example, tThe HTTP Inspect preprocessor decodes HTTP traffic, examining HTTP headers and payloads for anomalies or suspicious patterns. It can detect various web-based threats, such as cross-site scripting (XSS), SQL injection, and directory traversal attacks.

Anomaly Detection

Anomaly detection preprocessors identify deviations from normal network behavior, which can indicate potential threats. These preprocessors define baselines for expected traffic patterns and generate alerts when traffic deviates from these baselines.

For example, the Portscan preprocessor detects port scanning activities by identifying patterns consistent with reconnaissance techniques. It monitors network traffic for multiple connection attempts to different ports and generates alerts when suspicious scanning behavior is detected.

Traffic Reassembly

Traffic reassembly preprocessors handle packet fragmentation and TCP stream reassembly, allowing Snort to analyze complete sessions rather than individual packets. This capability is essential for detecting multi-packet attacks that span multiple segments.

For example, the Stream5 preprocessor reassembles TCP streams, allowing Snort to analyze entire sessions for potential threats. It identifies and reconstructs TCP streams, enabling the detection of attacks that occur across multiple segments, such as buffer overflow exploits or session hijacking attempts.

Popular Preprocessors In-use

Several preprocessors are commonly used in Snort to enhance its detection capabilities and address specific security challenges. Following are some of the most popular preprocessors and their functions:

Frag3 Preprocessor

The Frag3 preprocessor is responsible for handling IP fragmentation, reconstructing fragmented packets into complete datagrams for analysis. It detects and alerts on fragmentation-based evasion techniques, such as overlapping fragments or excessive fragmentation, which attackers use to bypass intrusion detection systems.

Key functions of Frag3:

- Reassembles fragmented IP packets for comprehensive analysis.
- Identifies fragmentation-based evasion techniques and generates alerts.
- Configurable parameters for fragment timeout and maximum fragment tracking.

Given below is a quick example of this configuration:

```
preprocessor frag3_engine: policy windows
detect_anomalies

preprocessor frag3_engine: policy first detect_anomalies
```

Stream5 Preprocessor

The Stream5 preprocessor is responsible for TCP stream reassembly, allowing Snort to analyze complete sessions rather than individual packets. It identifies and reconstructs TCP streams, enabling the detection of attacks that occur across multiple segments, such as buffer overflow exploits or session hijacking attempts.

Key functions of Stream5:

- Reassembles TCP streams for comprehensive analysis.
- Detects stream-based attacks and anomalies.
- Configurable parameters for session tracking and timeout.

Given below is a quick example of this configuration:

```
preprocessor stream5_global: max_tcp 8192, track_tcp yes

preprocessor stream5_tcp: policy windows, ports both 80
443 8080
```

HTTP Inspect Preprocessor

The HTTP Inspect preprocessor analyzes HTTP traffic, examining HTTP headers and payloads for anomalies or suspicious patterns. It can detect various web-based threats, such as cross-site scripting (XSS), SQL injection, and directory traversal attacks.

Key functions of HTTP Inspect:

- Decodes HTTP traffic and identifies protocol-specific anomalies.
- Detects web-based threats and generates alerts.
- Configurable parameters for HTTP normalization and inspection.

Given below is a quick example of this configuration:

```
preprocessor http_inspect: global iis_unicode_map
unicode.map 1252

preprocessor http_inspect_server: server default profile
all ports { 80 8080 3128 }
```

DNS Preprocessor

The DNS preprocessor analyzes DNS traffic to detect DNS-based attacks, such as DNS tunneling, cache poisoning, and DNS amplification attacks. It inspects DNS queries and responses for suspicious patterns and anomalies, enabling Snort to detect and respond to DNS-related threats effectively.

Key functions of DNS:

- Analyzes DNS traffic for protocol-specific anomalies and threats.
- Detects DNS-based attacks and generates alerts.

- Configurable parameters for DNS inspection and anomaly detection.

Given below is a quick example of this configuration:

```
preprocessor dns_inspect: ports { 53 } enable_rdata yes
```

Portscan Preprocessor

The Portscan preprocessor detects port scanning activities by identifying patterns consistent with reconnaissance techniques. It monitors network traffic for multiple connection attempts to different ports and generates alerts when suspicious scanning behavior is detected.

Key functions of Portscan:

- Detects port scanning activities and generates alerts.
- Configurable parameters for scan detection sensitivity and alerting.

Given below is a quick example of this configuration:

```
preprocessor sfportscan: proto  { all } memcap { 10000000
} sense_level { medium }
```

SSL Preprocessor

The SSL preprocessor inspects encrypted SSL/TLS traffic, allowing Snort to detect threats that occur within encrypted sessions. It performs tasks such as decrypting SSL/TLS traffic, analyzing SSL handshake messages, and identifying suspicious SSL certificate anomalies.

Key functions of SSL:

- Analyzes SSL/TLS traffic for protocol-specific anomalies and threats.
- Detects encrypted threats and generates alerts.
- Configurable parameters for SSL inspection and decryption.

Given below is a quick example of this configuration:

```
preprocessor ssl: ports { 443 8443 } trustservers no
```

SSH Preprocessor

The SSH preprocessor analyzes SSH traffic to detect SSH-based attacks, such as brute force attempts or unauthorized access. It inspects SSH sessions for suspicious patterns and anomalies, enabling Snort to detect and respond to SSH-related threats effectively.

Key functions of SSH:

- Analyzes SSH traffic for protocol-specific anomalies and threats.
- Detects SSH-based attacks and generates alerts.
- Configurable parameters for SSH inspection and anomaly detection.

Given below is a quick example of this configuration:

```
preprocessor ssh: server_ports { 22 2222 }
```

SMTP Preprocessor

The SMTP preprocessor analyzes SMTP traffic to detect email-based threats, such as spam, phishing, or malware distribution. It inspects SMTP sessions for suspicious patterns and anomalies, enabling Snort to detect and respond to email-related threats effectively.

Key functions of SMTP:

- Analyzes SMTP traffic for protocol-specific anomalies and threats.
- Detects email-based attacks and generates alerts.
- Configurable parameters for SMTP inspection and anomaly detection.

Given below is a quick example of this configuration:

```
preprocessor smtp: ports { 25 587 }
```

Configuring and Tuning Preprocessors

Accessing Preprocessor Configuration Settings

Preprocessors in Snort are configured through the main Snort configuration file, typically located at **/etc/snort/snort.lua**. This file contains various preprocessor directives that specify the settings and options for each preprocessor. To access and modify these settings, you need to edit the Snort configuration file.

To editing the Snort configuration file,

- Use a text editor to open the Snort configuration file:

```
sudo nano /etc/snort/snort.lua
```

- Scroll through the configuration file to find the preprocessor directives. Each preprocessor has a specific section with its configuration settings.
- Edit the preprocessor settings according to your requirements. Each preprocessor

directive includes parameters that can be adjusted to customize its behavior.

- After making the necessary changes, save the configuration file and exit the text editor.
- Restart Snort to apply the changes to the configuration:

```
sudo systemctl restart snort
```

Configuring Common Preprocessors

We will explore how to configure some of the commonly used preprocessors in Snort, focusing on their configuration settings and options.

Frag3 Preprocessor

The Frag3 preprocessor is configured as below:

```
preprocessor frag3_engine: policy first detect_anomalies
overlap_limit 10
```

In the given configuration option:

- Policy specifies the reassembly policy for fragmented packets. Common policies include **`first`**, **`last`**, and **`linux`**.
- Detect Anomalies will enable detection of fragmentation anomalies.
- And, the Overlap Limit sets the maximum number of overlapping fragments allowed.

Stream5 Preprocessor

The Stream5 preprocessor is configured as below:

```
preprocessor stream5_global: track_tcp yes, max_tcp 8192

preprocessor stream5_tcp: policy windows,
use_static_footprint_sizes
```

In the given configuration option:

- Track TCP enables tracking of TCP sessions for reassembly.
- Max TCP sets the maximum number of concurrent TCP sessions.
- Use Static Footprint Sizes optimizes memory usage for session tracking.

HTTP Inspect Preprocessor

The HTTP Inspect preprocessor analyzes HTTP traffic, inspecting headers and payloads for anomalies or suspicious patterns and it is configured as below:

```
preprocessor http_inspect: global iis_unicode_map
unicode.map 1252

preprocessor http_inspect_server: server default profile
all ports { 80 8080 }
```

In the given configuration option:

- IIS Unicode Map specifies the Unicode map file for decoding HTTP traffic.
- Profile defines the inspection profile, which includes settings for normalization and detection.
- And, the Ports list the ports where HTTP inspection is applied.

DNS Preprocessor

The DNS preprocessor is configured as below:

```
preprocessor dns_inspect: ports { 53 } enable_rdata yes
```

In the given configuration option, Enable RDATA enables inspection of DNS resource data for anomalies.

Tuning Preprocessors for Different Scenarios

Tuning preprocessors involves adjusting their settings to optimize performance and detection capabilities for specific network environments and threat scenarios. Different scenarios may require different tuning strategies to address unique challenges and security requirements.

High Traffic Volume

In high-traffic environments, Snort may experience performance issues if preprocessors are not tuned properly. Following are the ways of managing high traffic volumes:

- Increase Memory Limits

Adjust memory-related settings, such as **max_tcp** in the Stream5 preprocessor, to handle higher volumes of traffic:

```
preprocessor stream5_global: max_tcp 16384
```

- Optimize Session Tracking

Use static footprint sizes for session tracking to optimize memory usage:

```
preprocessor stream5_tcp: use_static_footprint_sizes
```

- Adjust Timeouts

Reduce session and fragment timeouts to free up resources more quickly:

```
preprocessor stream5_tcp: timeout 30

preprocessor frag3_engine: timeout 60
```

Complex Network Protocols

Complex network protocols, such as HTTP or DNS, may require specific tuning to ensure accurate detection and analysis. Following are the options:

- Enable Protocol-Specific Options

Enable options that enhance protocol analysis, such as inspecting HTTP headers or DNS resource data:

```
preprocessor http_inspect_server: enable_xff

preprocessor dns_inspect: enable_rdata yes
```

- Configure Protocol Profiles

Use protocol profiles to tailor inspection settings for specific protocols:

```
preprocessor http_inspect_server: profile apache
```

- Adjust Inspection Depth

Increase or decrease inspection depth based on protocol complexity and security requirements:

```
preprocessor http_inspect_server: max_header_length 1024
```

Evasion and Evasion Techniques

Attackers may use evasion techniques to bypass intrusion detection systems and to help detect and prevent these techniques, following strategies may work:

- Enable Anomaly Detection

Enable anomaly detection options to identify unusual patterns or behaviors:

```
preprocessor frag3_engine: detect_anomalies
```

- Configure Evasion Detection

Use options that detect evasion techniques, such as overlapping fragments or invalid sequences:

```
preprocessor frag3_engine: overlap_limit 10

preprocessor stream5_tcp: check_session_hijacking
```

- Adjust Fragmentation and Reassembly Settings

Configure fragmentation and reassembly settings to detect evasion techniques effectively:

```
preprocessor frag3_engine: min_ttl 5
```

Sample Program: Optimizing HTTP and TCP Preprocessors

We will walk through a practical example of tuning preprocessors for a web server environment that experiences high traffic volume and potential web-based threats. Suppose you are managing a web server environment with high traffic volume and potential web-based threats. So, the goal now is to optimize the HTTP Inspect and Stream5 preprocessors for efficient detection and performance.

HTTP Inspect Preprocessor

To begin with, first enable inspection of the X-Forwarded-For (XFF) header to identify client IP addresses behind proxies:

```
preprocessor http_inspect_server: server default
enable_xff
```

Then, set the maximum header length to accommodate large HTTP headers:

```
preprocessor http_inspect_server: max_header_length 2048
```

To decode Unicode-encoded HTTP traffic, use Unicode mapping:

```
preprocessor http_inspect: global iis_unicode_map
unicode.map 1252
```

Stream5 Preprocessor

Now, adjust the maximum number of concurrent TCP sessions to handle high traffic volume:

```
preprocessor stream5_global: max_tcp 16384
```

Optimize memory usage for session tracking:

```
preprocessor stream5_tcp: use_static_footprint_sizes
```

Enable the detection of session hijacking attempts:

```
preprocessor stream5_tcp: check_session_hijacking
```

DNS Preprocessor

Finally, inspect DNS resource data for anomalies:

```
preprocessor dns_inspect: enable_rdata yes
```

If you configure and tune these preprocessors, Snort will be able to handle large amounts of traffic more efficiently and detect web-based threats better.

Advanced Use of Preprocessor

Despite the fact that Snort comes with a number of preprocessors that are already built in, there may be circumstances in which you will need to write custom preprocessors in order to address particular security challenges or identify specific threat patterns. Furthermore, preprocessors can be used to detect protocol anomalies, which improves Snort's capability to detect complex threats that do not follow standard protocol behavior.

Writing Custom Preprocessors

Writing a custom preprocessor involves developing a module that integrates with Snort's processing pipeline and performs specific preprocessing tasks. Given below are quick steps to write a custom preprocessor:

1. Understand Snort's Preprocessor API

2. Define the Preprocessor's Purpose
3. Setup a Development Environment
4. Create the Preprocessor Module
5. Integrate with Snort
6. Compile and Test

We will walk through an example of creating a simple custom preprocessor that detects a specific pattern in network traffic and generates alerts. The preprocessor will detect a specific pattern in the packet payload, such as a string indicating a potential attack, and generate an alert.

Then, write the code for the preprocessor in C, implementing the initialization, packet processing, and cleanup functions.

```
#include <snort.h>


// Define the pattern to search for

static const char* pattern = "malicious_pattern";


// Initialization function

void my_preprocessor_init(void) {

    RegisterPreprocessor("my_preprocessor",
my_preprocessor_packet);

}


// Packet processing function

void my_preprocessor_packet(Packet* p) {

    if (p && p->payload) {

        // Search for the pattern in the packet payload
```

```
        if (strstr((char*)p->payload, pattern) != NULL) {
            // Generate an alert if the pattern is found
            SnortEvent alert;
            InitAlert(&alert, p);
            SetAlertMsg(&alert, "Custom Preprocessor:
Malicious Pattern Detected");
            Alert(&alert);
        }
    }
}

// Cleanup function
void my_preprocessor_cleanup(void) {
    // Perform any necessary cleanup tasks
}
```

Then, modify the Snort configuration file to load the custom preprocessor and specify any necessary settings.

```
preprocessor my_preprocessor
```

After that, compile Snort with the custom preprocessor included and test its functionality in a controlled environment. Once done, then generate network traffic containing the target pattern to verify that the preprocessor generates alerts as expected.

Implementing Preprocessors for Protocol Anomalies

Preprocessors can be implemented to detect protocol anomalies, which are deviations from expected protocol behavior that may indicate potential threats. Protocol anomalies occur when network traffic deviates from the expected behavior defined by a protocol's specifications. These anomalies can be indicative of various security threats, such as:

- Packets that do not conform to the protocol's structure or contain invalid fields.
- Traffic patterns that deviate from the expected sequence of protocol messages.
- Packet payloads that contain unexpected or suspicious data.

We will explore how to implement a preprocessor to detect anomalies in HTTP traffic. The preprocessor will analyze HTTP traffic and detect anomalies such as malformed HTTP requests or responses, unusual header values, and unexpected payloads.

Then, write the code for the preprocessor in C, implementing the necessary functions to analyze HTTP traffic and detect anomalies.

```
#include <snort.h>


// Initialization function

void http_anomaly_preprocessor_init(void) {

    RegisterPreprocessor("http_anomaly_preprocessor",
http_anomaly_packet);

}


// Packet processing function

void http_anomaly_packet(Packet* p) {

    if (p && p->payload) {

        // Analyze HTTP headers and payloads for
anomalies

        if (detect_malformed_http(p->payload)) {

            // Generate an alert for malformed HTTP
traffic
```

```
            SnortEvent alert;
            InitAlert(&alert, p);
            SetAlertMsg(&alert, "HTTP Anomaly Detected:
Malformed HTTP Request");
            Alert(&alert);
        }
        if (detect_unusual_payload(p->payload)) {
            // Generate an alert for unusual payloads
            SnortEvent alert;
            InitAlert(&alert, p);
            SetAlertMsg(&alert, "HTTP Anomaly Detected:
Unusual Payload");
            Alert(&alert);
        }
    }
}

// Helper function to detect malformed HTTP
int detect_malformed_http(const char* payload) {
    // Implement logic to detect malformed HTTP requests
or responses
    return 0; // Return 1 if anomaly is detected
```

```
}


// Helper function to detect unusual payloads
int detect_unusual_payload(const char* payload) {
    // Implement logic to detect unusual payloads
    return 0; // Return 1 if anomaly is detected
}


// Cleanup function
void http_anomaly_cleanup(void) {
    // Perform any necessary cleanup tasks
}
```

After this, modify the Snort configuration file to load the preprocessor and specify any necessary settings.

```
preprocessor http_anomaly_preprocessor
```

We will explore another example of implementing a preprocessor to detect anomalies in DNS traffic. In this, the preprocessor will analyze DNS traffic and detect anomalies such as malformed DNS queries or responses, unusual query types, and unexpected payload sizes.

```
#include <snort.h>


// Initialization function
void dns_anomaly_preprocessor_init(void) {
    RegisterPreprocessor("dns_anomaly_preprocessor",
```

```
dns_anomaly_packet);

}


// Packet processing function

void dns_anomaly_packet(Packet* p) {

    if (p && p->payload) {

        // Analyze DNS queries and responses for
anomalies

        if (detect_malformed_dns(p->payload)) {

            // Generate an alert for malformed DNS
traffic

            SnortEvent alert;

            InitAlert(&alert, p);

            SetAlertMsg(&alert, "DNS Anomaly Detected:
Malformed DNS Query");

            Alert(&alert);

        }

        if (detect_unusual_query_type(p->payload)) {

            // Generate an alert for unusual DNS query
types

            SnortEvent alert;

            InitAlert(&alert, p);

            SetAlertMsg(&alert, "DNS Anomaly Detected:
```

```
Unusual Query Type");
            Alert(&alert);
        }
    }
}

// Helper function to detect malformed DNS
int detect_malformed_dns(const char* payload) {
    // Implement logic to detect malformed DNS queries or
responses
    return 0; // Return 1 if anomaly is detected
}

// Helper function to detect unusual query types
int detect_unusual_query_type(const char* payload) {
    // Implement logic to detect unusual DNS query types
    return 0; // Return 1 if anomaly is detected
}

// Cleanup function
void dns_anomaly_cleanup(void) {
    // Perform any necessary cleanup tasks
```

```
}
```

And as usual, modify the Snort configuration file to load the preprocessor.

```
preprocessor dns_anomaly_preprocessor
```

It is possible to modify Snort to handle particular security needs and threat patterns by developing custom preprocessors. The implementation of preprocessors for protocol anomalies strengthens Snort's detection capabilities for complex attacks that depart from typical protocol behavior. This, in turn, provides strong defense against various threats.

Event Processing and Output Plugins

Configuring Output Modules

Output modules in Snort define how alerts and other event data are recorded, stored, and processed. Configuring output modules allows you to customize the way Snort logs and reports detected events, enabling efficient analysis and response to security incidents.

Now, to access the Snort configuration file:

- Use a text editor to open the Snort configuration file, typically located at **/etc/snort/snort.lua**:

```
sudo nano /etc/snort/snort.lua
```

- Scroll through the configuration file to find the output module directives. Each directive specifies the settings and options for a particular output module.
- Edit the output module settings according to your requirements. Each module includes parameters that can be adjusted to customize its behavior.
- After making the necessary changes, save the configuration file and exit the text editor.
- Then finally, restart Snort to apply the changes to the configuration

```
sudo systemctl restart snort
```

Snort also supports various output formats, each serving different purposes and use cases. Unified2 is a popular output format that provides efficient binary logging of Snort alerts and events, enabling integration with other analysis tools.

We will explore how to use Unified2 and other output formats.

Using Unified2

Unified2 is a binary output format that consolidates Snort alerts and events into a single file. This format is designed for high-performance logging and is commonly used for integration with external analysis tools, such as Barnyard2 and SIEM systems.

To configure Snort to use the Unified2 output format, add the following directive to the Snort configuration file

```
output unified2: filename snort.log, limit 128
```

In the given configuration option:

- Filename specifies the base name for Unified2 log files. Snort appends timestamps and sequence numbers to create unique filenames.
- And, Limit sets the maximum size of Unified2 log files in megabytes. When the limit is reached, Snort rotates the log file and creates a new one.

Given below are the advantages of Unified2:

- Unified2 provides efficient binary logging, reducing disk I/O and improving performance.
- Unified2 is compatible with various analysis tools, enabling seamless integration and correlation of Snort data.
- Unified2 supports large-scale deployments by handling high volumes of alerts and events.

Barnyard2 with Unified2

Barnyard2 is a popular tool for processing Unified2 output files and sending alerts to various destinations, such as databases and SIEM systems. To use Barnyard2 with Unified2, follow these steps:

Install Barnyard2

Install Barnyard2 on your system. This may require downloading and compiling the source code or using package management tools.

Configure Barnyard2

Create a configuration file for Barnyard2, specifying the input and output plugins. Following is the example configuration (**barnyard2.conf**):

```
config reference_file:      /etc/snort/reference.config
```

```
config classification_file:
/etc/snort/classification.config

config gen_file:                /etc/snort/gen-msg.map

config sid_file:                /etc/snort/sid-msg.map



input unified2

output database: log, mysql, user=snort dbname=snort
host=localhost password=yourpassword
```

Run Barnyard2

Execute Barnyard2 with the configuration file, specifying the Unified2 log directory and waldo file for tracking processed files:

```
sudo barnyard2 -c /etc/snort/barnyard2.conf -d
/var/log/snort/ -f snort.log -w
/var/log/snort/barnyard2.waldo
```

In the above code snippet,

- **-c** specifies the configuration file for Barnyard2.
- **-d** specifies the directory where Snort's Unified2 files are stored.
- **-f** specifies the base name of the Unified2 files.
- **-w** specifies the Waldo file for tracking processed files.

Using Other Output Formats

In addition to Unified2, Snort supports various other output formats, each offering different features and capabilities. Given below are some commonly used output formats:

Syslog Output Format

The Syslog output format sends Snort alerts and events to a Syslog server, allowing for centralized logging and monitoring of security incidents. To configure Snort to use the Syslog output format, add the following directive to the Snort configuration file:

```
output alert_syslog: LOG_AUTH LOG_ALERT
```

In the given configuration option:

- Facility specifies the Syslog facility to use, such as **LOG_AUTH** for authentication-related messages.
- Priority sets the Syslog priority level, such as **LOG_ALERT** for critical alerts.

Given below are the advantages of Syslog:

- Syslog enables centralized collection and analysis of logs from multiple sources, providing a comprehensive view of security events.
- Syslog is widely supported by various logging and monitoring tools, enabling seamless integration with existing infrastructure.

CSV Output Format

The CSV output format logs Snort alerts and events in a comma-separated values (CSV) format, making it easy to import and analyze data in spreadsheet applications. To configure Snort to use the CSV output format, add the following directive to the Snort configuration file:

```
output alert_csv: /var/log/snort/alert.csv
timestamp,sig_id,sig_rev,msg
```

In the given configuration option:

- Filename specifies the name of the CSV file where alerts are logged.
- Fields lists the fields to include in the CSV output, such as **timestamp**, **sig_id**, **sig_rev**, and **msg**.

Fast Alert Format

The Fast Alert format provides a simplified, concise alert format that is easy to read and parse. It is useful for environments where quick alert analysis is essential. To configure Snort to use the Fast Alert format, add the following directive to the Snort configuration file:

```
output alert_fast: /var/log/snort/alert.fast
```

Advantages of Fast Alert:

- Fast alerts provide a straightforward, easy-to-read format that is ideal for quick analysis and review.
- The simplified format reduces processing overhead, improving performance in high-

traffic environments.

JSON Output Format

The JSON output format logs Snort alerts and events in a structured JSON format, facilitating integration with modern logging and analysis tools. To configure Snort to use the JSON output format, add the following directive to the Snort configuration file:

```
output alert_json: /var/log/snort/alert.json
```

Advantages of JSON:

- JSON provides a structured format that is easy to parse and analyze with various programming languages and tools.
- JSON is compatible with many modern logging and analysis platforms, enabling seamless integration and analysis.

Sample Program: Configuring Unified2, Syslog, and JSON

We will walk through a practical example of configuring Snort to use multiple output formats to handle alerts and events efficiently. Suppose you want to configure Snort to log alerts in Unified2, Syslog, and JSON formats to ensure comprehensive logging and analysis capabilities.

Configure Unified2 Output

Add the following directive to the Snort configuration file to enable Unified2 output:

```
output unified2: filename snort.log, limit 128
```

Configure Syslog Output

Add the following directive to the Snort configuration file to enable Syslog output:

```
output alert_syslog: LOG_AUTH LOG_ALERT
```

Configure JSON Output

Add the following directive to the Snort configuration file to enable JSON output:

```
output alert_json: /var/log/snort/alert.json
```

Then, restart Snort to apply the changes to the configuration:

```
sudo systemctl restart snort
```

Verify Logging

Generate test traffic to trigger Snort alerts and verify that alerts are logged in the specified formats:

- Check the **/var/log/snort/** directory for Unified2 log files.
- Check the Syslog server or **/var/log/syslog** file for Snort alerts.
- Check the **/var/log/snort/alert.json** file for JSON-formatted alerts.

By leveraging formats like Unified2, Syslog, CSV, Fast Alert, and JSON, you can customize Snort's logging and alerting capabilities to meet your specific needs and integrate with existing analysis tools and platforms.

Summary

In sum, the advanced features of Snort's preprocessors and event processing were covered in this chapter. It began with Snort preprocessors, explaining how they normalize data, analyze protocols, detect anomalies, and reassemble fragmented packets before they reach Snort's detection engine. Various preprocessors, including Frag3, Stream5, HTTP Inspect, DNS, Portscan, and others, were explored, with a focus on their functionality and configurations.

The chapter then looked at configuring and tuning preprocessors to improve Snort's performance and detection capabilities. It taught how to read the Snort configuration file for preprocessor settings, how to change parameters to fit various network environments, and how to tune preprocessors for situations like heavy traffic, complicated protocols, and evasion methods. We also took a look at advanced preprocessor usage, including how to write your own preprocessors. This entailed learning Snort's preprocessor API, defining the purpose of custom preprocessors, and developing modules for detecting protocol anomalies.

Finally, the chapter covered event processing and output plugins, showing how to set up output modules and use different output formats such as Unified2, Syslog, CSV, Fast Alert, and JSON. Unified2 was recognized for its efficient binary logging and compatibility with data analysis tools such as Barnyard2. Other formats, such as Syslog and JSON, provided structured logging options for integration into various logging systems and platforms. Overall, this chapter provided us a thorough understanding of preprocessors and event processing to optimize Snort for robust intrusion detection and response.

CHAPTER 6: LEVERAGING DYNAMIC MODULES AND PLUGINS

Chapter Overview

In this chapter, we look at Snort's powerful dynamic modules and plugins, which enable flexible and scalable intrusion detection solutions. This chapter begins by explaining how dynamic modules improve Snort's detection capabilities and how they differ from traditional static rules. We will then look at working with dynamic rules and libraries, which are critical components of Snort's dynamic module system. You will learn how to load and manage dynamic rules, as well as how to use shared libraries to improve Snort's detection of complex threats. This section will walk you through the process of configuring and deploying dynamic modules to meet specific security requirements.

The chapter also practically demonstrates the creation of custom Snort modules, including insights into custom detection logic and integration with Snort's processing pipeline. This will entail analyzing Snort's module development framework and implementing the necessary APIs and tools. Finally, we will look at testing and debugging modules, emphasizing the importance of validating custom modules to ensure they work properly and effectively. You will learn how to identify and resolve issues in dynamic modules, ensuring optimal performance and reliability.

Understanding Dynamic Modules

Dynamic modules in Snort are extensions that enhance its capabilities by providing additional detection logic, preprocessors, or output functionalities. These modules are loaded at runtime and allow Snort to be highly customizable and adaptable to evolving security threats. Dynamic modules offer flexibility by enabling you to integrate new features and functionalities without modifying Snort's core codebase. This section will explore the types of dynamic modules and demonstrate how to integrate third-party modules into Snort.

Types of Dynamic Modules

Dynamic modules in Snort can be categorized into several types based on their functions and the enhancements they provide. Understanding these types is essential for effectively leveraging dynamic modules to address specific security needs.

Dynamic Preprocessor Modules

Dynamic preprocessor modules extend Snort's preprocessing capabilities by adding new preprocessors that analyze and manipulate network traffic before it reaches the detection engine. These modules can handle specific protocols, normalize traffic, or detect anomalies that standard preprocessors might miss.

For example, a dynamic preprocessor module could be developed to analyze a new protocol or enhance the capabilities of an existing protocol preprocessor, such as detecting additional anomalies in HTTP or DNS traffic.

Dynamic Detection Modules

Dynamic detection modules extend Snort's detection capabilities by providing additional detection logic or rules. These modules can be used to implement complex detection algorithms or integrate specialized threat intelligence feeds into Snort's detection engine.

For example, a dynamic detection module might implement a machine learning algorithm to identify unusual patterns in network traffic, providing advanced threat detection capabilities beyond traditional signature-based methods.

Dynamic Output Modules

Dynamic output modules extend Snort's ability to log and report alerts and events. These modules can integrate with third-party logging systems, databases, or SIEM platforms, providing enhanced event processing and analysis capabilities.

For example, a dynamic output module could send Snort alerts to a centralized logging server or SIEM system in a specific format, enabling seamless integration with existing security infrastructure.

Integrating Third-Party Modules

Integrating third-party modules into Snort allows you to extend its functionality and its integration involves downloading, configuring, and loading the modules into Snort. To illustrate the integration process, we will walk through an example of integrating a third-party dynamic detection module into Snort. This module will add custom detection logic for a specific threat type.

Identify and Download the Module

Begin by identifying the third-party module you wish to integrate. This module might be available from a security vendor, open-source community, or GitHub repository. Download the module's source code or precompiled binary package.

```
wget https://gitforgits.com/snort-
modules/custom_detection_module.tar.gz
```

Extract the downloaded package:

```
tar -xzvf custom_detection_module.tar.gz
```

If the module is provided as source code, compile and build it to create the dynamic library files. Here, ensure you have the necessary development tools and dependencies installed. First, navigate to the module's directory:

```
cd custom_detection_module
```

Compile and build the module:

```
./configure

make

sudo make install
```

The build process generates a dynamic library file, typically with a **.so** extension, which can be loaded into Snort.

Configure Snort to Load the Module

Modify the Snort configuration file to load the dynamic module. The configuration file, usually located at **/etc/snort/snort.lua**, needs to be updated to include the module. Open the Snort configuration file using a text editor:

```
sudo nano /etc/snort/snort.lua
```

Add a directive to load the dynamic module:

```
dynamic_detection_library
/usr/local/lib/snort_dynamicrules/custom_detection_module
.so
```

However, specify any additional configuration options or parameters required by the module. These options are usually documented in the module's documentation or README file.

Verify Module Loading

After configuring Snort to load the dynamic module, verify that the module loads correctly without errors. Run Snort in test mode to check for any issues.

```
sudo snort -c /etc/snort/snort.lua -T
```

Look for messages indicating successful loading of the dynamic module. If there are errors, review the module's configuration settings and resolve any issues. Then, restart the Snort to apply the changes and activate the dynamic module:

```
sudo systemctl restart snort
```

Test Module Functionality

Generate network traffic that should trigger the module's detection logic and verify that it functions as expected. Check Snort's alert logs or output to confirm that the module is detecting and reporting events correctly.

```
tail -f /var/log/snort/alert
```

And then you may proceed to analyze the logs to verify that the custom detection module is generating alerts for the specified threat type.

Sample Program: Integrating a Dynamic Preprocessor Module

We will explore an example of integrating a dynamic preprocessor module that detects anomalies in a specific protocol, such as SSH.

First, identify a dynamic preprocessor module designed to enhance SSH protocol analysis and download it from a trusted source.

```
wget https://gitforgits.com/snort-
modules/ssh_anomaly_preprocessor.tar.gz
```

Extract the downloaded package:

```
tar -xzvf ssh_anomaly_preprocessor.tar.gz
```

Navigate to the module's directory:

```
cd ssh_anomaly_preprocessor
```

Compile and build the module:

```
./configure

make

sudo make install
```

The build process generates a dynamic library file for the preprocessor. Modify the Snort configuration file to load the dynamic preprocessor module. For this, open the configuration file:

```
sudo nano /etc/snort/snort.lua
```

Add a directive to load the dynamic preprocessor module:

```
dynamic_preprocessor
/usr/local/lib/snort_dynamicpreproc/ssh_anomaly_preproces
sor.so
```

Then, run Snort in test mode to verify that the preprocessor module loads successfully:

```
sudo snort -c /etc/snort/snort.lua -T
```

Restart Snort to apply the changes and activate the preprocessor module:

```
sudo systemctl restart snort
```

By learning how to integrate third-party modules and configure Snort to load them, you can enhance Snort's performance and tailor it.

Working with Dynamic Rules and Libraries

Background

Dynamic rules and libraries in Snort provide a flexible and scalable approach to extend its detection capabilities beyond static rules. Dynamic rules allow you to create rules that can change their behavior or criteria based on external data or conditions, while dynamic libraries offer a way to encapsulate complex detection logic or algorithms. This section will take you through the process of writing dynamic rules and developing custom dynamic libraries to enhance Snort's functionality.

Dynamic rules in Snort are designed to respond to changing conditions or incorporate external intelligence into the detection process. Unlike static rules, which are fixed and predefined, dynamic rules can adapt their behavior based on external data sources or runtime conditions. Dynamic rules are typically implemented through dynamic detection modules and scripts that provide flexibility and adaptability.

They may include the following components:

1. External Data Sources: Dynamic rules can reference external data, such as threat intelligence feeds or custom databases, to adjust their detection criteria dynamically.

2. Scripts or Code Logic: Dynamic rules often include scripts or code logic that evaluates conditions, manipulates data, or triggers actions based on specified criteria.
3. Dynamic Detection Modules: These modules provide the framework for executing dynamic rules and integrating them with Snort's detection engine.

Writing Dynamic Rule to Integrate Threat Intelligence

We will explore an example of creating a dynamic rule that integrates threat intelligence data to detect IP addresses associated with known threats.

Setup External Data Source

Begin by setting up an external data source, such as a threat intelligence feed or custom database, containing IP addresses associated with known threats. This data source will be used by the dynamic rule to adjust its detection criteria.

Create a file named **threat_intel.txt** containing a list of known malicious IP addresses:

```
192.168.1.100

10.0.0.200

203.0.113.5
```

Develop Dynamic Detection Module

Write a dynamic detection module that loads the external data source and evaluates incoming traffic against it. This module will generate alerts for traffic originating from or destined for known malicious IP addresses.

```
#include <snort.h>

#include <stdio.h>

#include <string.h>



// Define the maximum number of IP addresses to track

#define MAX_IPS 1000
```

```
// Array to store known malicious IP addresses
static char* malicious_ips[MAX_IPS];
static int ip_count = 0;

// Function to load IP addresses from the external data
source
void load_threat_intel() {
    FILE* file = fopen("/etc/snort/threat_intel.txt",
"r");
    if (!file) {
        perror("Failed to open threat intelligence
file");
        return;
    }
    char line[256];
    while (fgets(line, sizeof(line), file) && ip_count <
MAX_IPS) {
        line[strcspn(line, "\n")] = 0; // Remove newline
character
        malicious_ips[ip_count++] = strdup(line);
    }
    fclose(file);
}
```

```
// Initialization function for the dynamic detection
module
void dynamic_detection_init(void) {
    RegisterPreprocessor("dynamic_detection",
dynamic_detection_packet);
    load_threat_intel();
}

// Packet processing function for the dynamic detection
module
void dynamic_detection_packet(Packet* p) {
    if (!p || !p->iph) return;

    char src_ip[16], dst_ip[16];
    snprintf(src_ip, sizeof(src_ip), "%s", inet_ntoa(p-
>iph->ip_src));
    snprintf(dst_ip, sizeof(dst_ip), "%s", inet_ntoa(p-
>iph->ip_dst));

    // Check if the packet source or destination matches
known malicious IPs
    for (int i = 0; i < ip_count; i++) {
        if (strcmp(src_ip, malicious_ips[i]) == 0 ||
```

```
strcmp(dst_ip, malicious_ips[i]) == 0) {
            // Generate an alert for matching traffic
            SnortEvent alert;
            InitAlert(&alert, p);
            SetAlertMsg(&alert, "Dynamic Rule: Traffic
to/from Known Malicious IP Detected");
            Alert(&alert);
            break;
        }
    }
}

// Cleanup function for the dynamic detection module
void dynamic_detection_cleanup(void) {
    for (int i = 0; i < ip_count; i++) {
        free(malicious_ips[i]);
    }
}
```

Integrate the Module with Snort

Compile the dynamic detection module and integrate it with Snort. Modify the Snort configuration file to load the module.

```
gcc -fPIC -shared -o dynamic_detection.so
dynamic_detection.c
```

```
sudo mv dynamic_detection.so
/usr/local/lib/snort_dynamicrules/
```

Open the Snort configuration file:

```
sudo nano /etc/snort/snort.lua
```

Add a directive to load the dynamic detection module:

```
dynamic_detection_library
/usr/local/lib/snort_dynamicrules/dynamic_detection.so
```

Verify and Test

Run Snort in test mode to verify the successful loading of the dynamic detection module:

```
sudo snort -c /etc/snort/snort.lua -T
```

Restart Snort and generate test traffic to verify the module's functionality:

```
sudo systemctl restart snort

tail -f /var/log/snort/alert
```

Check the logs for alerts indicating traffic to or from known malicious IP addresses.

Developing Custom Dynamic Libraries

Custom dynamic libraries in Snort encapsulate complex detection logic or algorithms, allowing for advanced threat detection capabilities. These libraries can be developed to extend Snort's functionality and provide custom processing logic that integrates seamlessly with Snort's detection engine.

First, determine the specific functionality or detection logic the dynamic library will provide. This could include implementing a custom detection algorithm, integrating external data sources, or enhancing existing Snort capabilities. Suppose you want to develop a custom protocol analyzer library that analyzes a proprietary protocol and detects anomalies as below:

```
#include <snort.h>
```

```
// Define the proprietary protocol structure
typedef struct {
    uint16_t header;
    uint16_t length;
    uint8_t payload[256];
} proprietary_protocol_t;

// Function to analyze the proprietary protocol
int analyze_protocol(const uint8_t* data, int len) {
    if (len < sizeof(proprietary_protocol_t)) return 0;

    const proprietary_protocol_t* packet = (const
proprietary_protocol_t*)data;

    // Perform custom analysis on the protocol
    if (packet->header != 0xABCD || packet->length >
sizeof(packet->payload)) {
        return 1; // Anomaly detected
    }
    return 0; // No anomaly detected
}
```

```
// Packet processing function for the custom library
void custom_protocol_packet(Packet* p) {
    if (!p || !p->payload || !p->dsize) return;

    if (analyze_protocol(p->payload, p->dsize)) {
        // Generate an alert for protocol anomalies
        SnortEvent alert;
        InitAlert(&alert, p);
        SetAlertMsg(&alert, "Custom Protocol Analyzer:
Protocol Anomaly Detected");
        Alert(&alert);
    }
}

// Initialization function for the custom library
void custom_protocol_init(void) {
    RegisterPreprocessor("custom_protocol_analyzer",
custom_protocol_packet);
}

// Cleanup function for the custom library
void custom_protocol_cleanup(void) {
```

```
    // Perform any necessary cleanup tasks
}
```

Then, compile and build the dynamic library from the source code:

```
gcc -fPIC -shared -o custom_protocol_analyzer.so
custom_protocol_analyzer.c

sudo mv custom_protocol_analyzer.so
/usr/local/lib/snort_dynamicrules/
```

Then, modify the Snort configuration file to load the custom dynamic library:

```
sudo nano /etc/snort/snort.lua
```

Later, add a directive to load the custom library:

```
dynamic_preprocessor
/usr/local/lib/snort_dynamicrules/custom_protocol_analyze
r.so
```

Finally, run the Snort in test mode to verify the successful loading of the custom dynamic library:

```
sudo snort -c /etc/snort/snort.lua -T
```

Restart Snort and generate test traffic to verify the library's functionality:

```
sudo systemctl restart snort

tail -f /var/log/snort/alert
```

If required, check the logs for alerts indicating protocol anomalies detected by the custom library.

Developing Custom Snort Modules

Custom modules allow you to implement specialized detection logic, preprocessors, or output functionalities that are not covered by existing Snort features. In this section, we will demonstrate you through the process of developing custom Snort modules, from creating and compiling them to integrating them into your existing Snort deployment.

Creating Custom Snort Modules

Following is a step-by-step demonstration to create a custom Snort module.

Define the Module's Purpose

The first step in developing a custom module is to define its purpose and functionality. Determine what specific task or detection logic the module will perform. This could include analyzing a specific protocol, detecting unusual patterns, or integrating with an external system.

Suppose you want to develop a custom module that detects anomalies in a proprietary network protocol used by your organization. The module will analyze packets for unexpected payload sizes and header values, generating alerts when anomalies are detected.

Setup a Development Environment

To create and compile a custom Snort module, you need a development environment with the necessary tools and libraries. This includes:

- A C/C++ compiler (e.g., GCC).
- The Snort source code for reference and integration.
- Necessary development libraries and headers (e.g., libpcap).

Install these tools on your system:

```
sudo apt-get install build-essential libpcap-dev
```

Write the Custom Module Code

Write the code and it should include the necessary functions to initialize the module, process packets, and clean up resources. Following is the example:

```
#include <snort.h>

#include <stdio.h>

#include <string.h>

#include <arpa/inet.h>
```

```c
// Define the proprietary protocol structure

typedef struct {

    uint16_t header;

    uint16_t length;

    uint8_t payload[256];

} proprietary_protocol_t;


// Function to analyze the proprietary protocol for
anomalies

int analyze_protocol(const uint8_t* data, int len) {

    if (len < sizeof(proprietary_protocol_t)) return 0;


    const proprietary_protocol_t* packet = (const
proprietary_protocol_t*)data;


    // Check for anomalies in the protocol header and
length

    if (packet->header != 0xABCD || packet->length >
sizeof(packet->payload)) {

        return 1; // Anomaly detected

    }

    return 0; // No anomaly detected

}
```

```
// Packet processing function for the custom module
void custom_protocol_packet(Packet* p) {
    if (!p || !p->payload || !p->dsize) return;

    if (analyze_protocol(p->payload, p->dsize)) {
        // Generate an alert for detected anomalies
        SnortEvent alert;
        InitAlert(&alert, p);
        SetAlertMsg(&alert, "Custom Protocol Anomaly
Detected");
        Alert(&alert);
    }
}

// Initialization function for the custom module
void custom_protocol_init(void) {
    RegisterPreprocessor("custom_protocol_analyzer",
custom_protocol_packet);
}

// Cleanup function for the custom module
```

```
void custom_protocol_cleanup(void) {
    // Perform any necessary cleanup tasks
}
```

In the above example,

- The code defines a structure representing the proprietary protocol with fields for the header, length, and payload.
- The **analyze_protocol** function checks for anomalies in the protocol, such as incorrect header values or payload lengths.
- The **custom_protocol_packet** function processes each packet, analyzing it for anomalies and generating alerts when issues are detected.
- The module includes functions for initialization and cleanup, registering the packet processing function with Snort.

Compile the Custom Module

Compile the custom module into a shared library that can be loaded by Snort. Use the following command to compile the code:

```
gcc -fPIC -shared -o custom_protocol_analyzer.so
custom_protocol_analyzer.c
```

This command generates a shared library file named **custom_protocol_analyzer.so**.

Integrate the Module into Snort

To integrate the custom module into Snort, you need to copy the compiled shared library to the appropriate directory and configure Snort to load it.

```
sudo cp custom_protocol_analyzer.so
/usr/local/lib/snort_dynamicpreproc/
```

Open the Snort configuration file using a text editor:

```
sudo nano /etc/snort/snort.lua
```

Add a directive to load the custom module:

```
dynamic_preprocessor
/usr/local/lib/snort_dynamicpreproc/custom_protocol_analy
zer.so
```

Then, run Snort in test mode to verify that the custom module loads successfully without errors:

```
sudo snort -c /etc/snort/snort.lua -T
```

Restart Snort to apply the changes and activate the custom module:

```
sudo systemctl restart snort
```

Generate network traffic that should trigger the module's detection logic and verify that it functions as expected. Check Snort's alert logs or output to confirm that the module is detecting and reporting anomalies correctly.

```
tail -f /var/log/snort/alert
```

And then finally analyze the logs to verify that the custom module is generating alerts for protocol anomalies or not.

Sample Program: Developing Custom Module for HTTP Anomaly Detection

We will explore another example of developing a custom module that detects anomalies in HTTP traffic, such as unusual HTTP methods or malformed requests.

First, write the code for the HTTP anomaly detection module:

```
#include <snort.h>

#include <stdio.h>

#include <string.h>



// Function to analyze HTTP requests for anomalies

int analyze_http(const uint8_t* data, int len) {
```

```
    if (len < 4) return 0; // Minimum length for HTTP
method

    // Check for unusual HTTP methods
    if (strncmp((char*)data, "UNUSUAL", 7) == 0) {
        return 1; // Anomaly detected
    }
    // Check for malformed requests
    if (strchr((char*)data, '\n') == NULL) {
        return 1; // Anomaly detected
    }
    return 0; // No anomaly detected
}

// Packet processing function for the HTTP anomaly
detection module
void http_anomaly_packet(Packet* p) {
    if (!p || !p->payload || !p->dsize) return;

    if (analyze_http(p->payload, p->dsize)) {
        // Generate an alert for detected anomalies
        SnortEvent alert;
```

```
        InitAlert(&alert, p);

        SetAlertMsg(&alert, "HTTP Anomaly Detected");

        Alert(&alert);

    }

}


// Initialization function for the HTTP anomaly detection
module

void http_anomaly_init(void) {

    RegisterPreprocessor("http_anomaly_analyzer",
http_anomaly_packet);

}


// Cleanup function for the HTTP anomaly detection module

void http_anomaly_cleanup(void) {

    // Perform any necessary cleanup tasks

}
```

In the above code,

- The **analyze_http** function checks for anomalies in HTTP requests, such as unusual methods (**"UNUSUAL"**) or malformed requests lacking newline characters.
- The **http_anomaly_packet** function processes each packet, analyzing it for HTTP anomalies and generating alerts when issues are detected.

Then, compile the module into a shared library:

```
gcc -fPIC -shared -o http_anomaly_analyzer.so
```

```
http_anomaly_analyzer.c
```

After that, copy the compiled shared library to the appropriate directory:

```
sudo cp http_anomaly_analyzer.so
/usr/local/lib/snort_dynamicpreproc/
```

Modify the Snort configuration file to load the module:

```
sudo nano /etc/snort/snort.lua
```

Add the directive:

```
dynamic_preprocessor
/usr/local/lib/snort_dynamicpreproc/http_anomaly_analyzer
.so
```

Run Snort in test mode to verify successful loading of the module:

```
sudo snort -c /etc/snort/snort.lua -T
```

Restart Snort and generate test traffic to verify the module's functionality:

```
sudo systemctl restart snort

tail -f /var/log/snort/alert
```

Check the logs for alerts indicating HTTP anomalies detected by the custom module. Overall, developing the custom Snort modules provides a powerful way to extend Snort's capabilities and address specific security challenges.

Testing and Debugging Modules

Validating the functionality of so far developed modules involves verifying that they detect the intended threats and perform their tasks as expected. Additionally, troubleshooting is essential for resolving issues that may arise during implementation, such as errors in module loading, performance bottlenecks, or incorrect detection logic. This section will instruct you through the process of testing, validating, and debugging custom Snort modules.

Once a custom module is created and integrated into Snort, it's essential to validate its functionality. Validation ensures that the module performs as intended and provides reliable detection capabilities.

Run Snort in Test Mode

Use Snort's test mode to verify that the custom module loads successfully and without errors. Test mode allows you to check the configuration and ensure that Snort recognizes and initializes the module correctly.

```
sudo snort -c /etc/snort/snort.lua -T
```

Look for output messages indicating successful loading of the module. Check for any warnings or errors that might indicate configuration issues or missing dependencies. Then, create test network traffic that should trigger the custom module's detection logic. This step involves crafting specific packets or using traffic generation tools to simulate scenarios that the module is designed to detect.

For a module that detects anomalies in a proprietary protocol, use a packet crafting tool like **scapy** to generate traffic with the expected anomalies.

```
from scapy.all import *



packet = Ether() / IP(dst="192.168.1.1") /
Raw(load=b"\xab\xcd\xff\xff\xff\xff\xff\xff")

sendp(packet, iface="eth0")
```

After this, assess the module's impact on Snort's performance, including processing speed and resource utilization. Monitor CPU and memory usage during testing to identify any performance bottlenecks introduced by the module.

If issues arise during testing or implementation, troubleshooting is necessary to identify and resolve the underlying problems. Common issues include module loading errors, incorrect detection logic, and performance bottlenecks.

Review Error Messages

Carefully review any error messages or warnings generated during Snort's initialization or runtime. Error messages can provide valuable clues about the source of the problem, such as syntax errors, missing dependencies, or incorrect configuration settings.

Example Error Message:

```
ERROR: Failed to load dynamic module
'/usr/local/lib/snort_dynamicrules/custom_protocol_analyz
er.so': undefined symbol: registerPreprocessor
```

This error indicates a missing or incorrectly referenced function, suggesting an issue with the module's code or build process.

Then, verify that all required dependencies for the custom module are installed and correctly referenced in the module's code. This includes libraries, headers, and any external resources the module relies on. After that, review the module's code logic to identify any errors or inefficiencies as given in the following snippet:

```
void custom_protocol_packet(Packet* p) {

    if (!p || !p->payload || !p->dsize) return;


    if (analyze_protocol(p->payload, p->dsize)) {

        SnortEvent alert;

        InitAlert(&alert, p);

        SetAlertMsg(&alert, "Custom Protocol Anomaly
Detected");

        Alert(&alert);

    }

}
```

Do check that the **analyze_protocol** function correctly handles packets with varying sizes and contents.

Then, add debugging output to the module's code to gain insights into its internal state and behavior. For example, you can insert print statements to output relevant information during packet processing as given below:

```
void custom_protocol_packet(Packet* p) {
```

```
    if (!p || !p->payload || !p->dsize) return;

    printf("Processing packet from %s to %s\n",
inet_ntoa(p->iph->ip_src), inet_ntoa(p->iph->ip_dst));

    if (analyze_protocol(p->payload, p->dsize)) {
        printf("Anomaly detected in packet\n");
        SnortEvent alert;
        InitAlert(&alert, p);
        SetAlertMsg(&alert, "Custom Protocol Anomaly
Detected");
        Alert(&alert);
    }
}
```

Compile the module with debugging output and run Snort to capture the output in the console.

You can then simplify the test conditions to isolate specific issues and confirm the module's basic functionality. This approach can help identify whether a particular aspect of the module or test environment is causing problems.

For example, you can temporarily remove complex detection logic and test the module with basic conditions as below:

```
if (p->dsize > 0) {
    printf("Packet detected with payload size: %d\n", p-
>dsize);
    SnortEvent alert;
```

```
    InitAlert(&alert, p);

    SetAlertMsg(&alert, "Basic Detection Triggered");

    Alert(&alert);

}
```

If issues persist, seek support from the Snort community, including forums, mailing lists, and online groups. Experienced developers can offer advice and solutions based on their expertise with Snort and module development. For example, post questions or issues on Snort forums or mailing lists to get assistance from the community as shown below:

```
Subject: Issue with Custom Snort Module Loading


Hi Snort Community,


I am experiencing an issue with loading a custom Snort
module that detects anomalies in a proprietary protocol.
The module compiles successfully, but Snort fails to load
it with an undefined symbol error. I have verified the
dependencies and reviewed the code logic but haven't
identified the source of the problem. Any insights or
suggestions would be greatly appreciated.


Thank you,

GitforGits
```

Testing and debugging custom Snort modules are essential steps in ensuring their reliability and effectiveness. By validating module functionality and troubleshooting any issues that arise, you can enhance Snort's capabilities and ensure robust detection of security threats. As you gain experience with testing and debugging, you'll be better equipped to develop high-quality custom modules that address specific security challenges and integrate seamlessly with Snort's detection engine.

Summary

In a nutshell, this chapter focused on using Snort's dynamic modules and plugins to improve its detection capabilities and adaptability to specific security requirements. At the outset of the chapter, the idea of dynamic modules was introduced. These modules enhance Snort's capabilities by incorporating personal detection logic, preprocessors, and output functionalities. Different types of dynamic modules, such as dynamic preprocessors, detection modules, and output modules, were explored, with a focus on their roles in enhancing Snort's processing pipeline.

The chapter then demonstrated how to write dynamic rules that incorporate external intelligence and create custom dynamic libraries to encapsulate complex detection logic. This included practical examples of developing dynamic detection modules and integrating them with Snort to detect specific threats. The chapter focused heavily on developing custom Snort modules, teaching how to write and compile custom modules to perform specialized detection tasks. It consisted of drafting code in C or C++, building it into shared libraries, and then incorporating these libraries into Snort's setup. Practical examples, such as developing modules for proprietary protocol analysis and HTTP anomaly detection, demonstrated how to extend Snort's capabilities using custom modules.

At the end of the chapter, we talked about testing and debugging modules, with an emphasis on how important it is to validate module functionality and fix problems. In order to test modules, we used methods like creating test traffic, keeping an eye on alerts, and seeing how it affected performance.And, to successfully identify and fix issues, troubleshooting techniques included reviewing error messages, checking dependencies, and enabling debugging output. As a whole, this chapter taught you how to build and administer your own Snort modules, which improved the security system's responsiveness to a wide range of threats.

Chapter 7: Deploying Snort in a Production Environment

Chapter Overview

Here we will go over all aspects of putting Snort into a production setting, with an emphasis on methods that have proven effective in the past for preventing intrusions. We start by looking at how to make a detailed plan for deploying Snort. Learners will be able to evaluate network designs, pinpoint monitoring hotspots, and ascertain what configurations and resources are required to achieve organizational security goals.

The chapter then delves into performance tuning and optimization, by learning how to fine-tune its configuration, manage resource allocation, and optimize detection rules. These strategies are critical for achieving peak performance in environments with varying traffic loads and security requirements. For Snort to function properly, high availability and failover must be in place. This section guides to set up multiple Snort systems in order to guarantee continuous protection and reduce downtime in the event of a failure. By understanding how clustering, load balancing, and failover work, you will be able to improve Snort's resilience and dependability.

Finally, the chapter teaches monitoring and managing Snort operations, emphasizing the value of proactive monitoring and maintenance. This includes configuring alerting and logging mechanisms, analyzing Snort output for insights, and running regular updates and audits.

Designing a Snort Deployment Plan

If you want Snort to meet your organization's security needs and accomplish its goals of intrusion detection and prevention, you need to plan ahead before deploying it to a production environment. To get the most out of Snort and make sure it fits in with your current network setup, you need a deployment plan. This section will go over the important things to think about when making a plan to deploy Snort and where to put the sensors so that your network is completely protected.

Key Considerations for Snort Deployment

Network Architecture Assessment

Assess the existing network topology, including the layout of devices, network segments, and critical assets. Identify the points where network traffic flows, such as routers, switches, firewalls, and gateways, to determine the optimal locations for placing Snort sensors. The goal is to position Snort in areas where it can monitor and analyze traffic most effectively.

Following are the considerations:

- Identify key network segments that require monitoring, such as DMZs, internal LANs, and external connections.
- Determine the network paths that carry sensitive or critical data, prioritizing these for

Snort deployment.

- Consider network choke points where traffic can be easily monitored without introducing bottlenecks.

Define Security Objectives

Clearly define the security objectives and goals for deploying Snort. This includes identifying the types of threats you want to detect, the level of protection required, and the acceptable trade-offs between performance and detection accuracy. Understanding these objectives will direct the configuration and tuning of Snort sensors to align with your organization's security policies.

Following are the considerations:

- Identify the types of threats relevant to your organization, such as malware, unauthorized access, or data exfiltration.
- Determine the acceptable level of risk and false positives, balancing detection sensitivity with operational efficiency.
- Consider compliance requirements and industry standards that may influence the deployment plan.

Resource Allocation and Sizing

Assess the resources available for deploying Snort, including hardware, software, and personnel. Ensure that the deployment plan accounts for the necessary computational power, storage, and network capacity to handle expected traffic loads and analysis requirements. Adequate resource allocation ensures that Snort operates efficiently without causing performance degradation.

Following are the considerations:

- Estimate the volume of network traffic to be analyzed and allocate sufficient processing power and memory.
- Determine storage requirements for logging and alert data, considering retention policies and analysis needs.
- Allocate personnel resources for managing and maintaining the Snort deployment, including monitoring, updates, and troubleshooting.

Scalability and Flexibility

Design the Snort deployment plan with scalability and flexibility in mind to accommodate future growth and changes in the network environment. A scalable deployment allows you to add or adjust Snort sensors as needed, ensuring continuous protection as your network evolves.

Following are the considerations:

- Plan for additional sensors or nodes to cover new network segments or increased traffic volumes.

- Implement modular configurations that allow for easy adjustments or additions to the Snort deployment.
- Consider virtualized or cloud-based Snort deployments to enable rapid scaling and flexibility.

Redundancy and Resilience

Ensure that the Snort deployment is resilient and capable of maintaining operations during failures or disruptions. Redundancy measures, such as failover configurations and backup sensors, help minimize downtime and maintain continuous security coverage.

Following are the considerations:

- Implement failover mechanisms to switch traffic analysis to backup sensors during hardware or software failures.
- Use load balancing to distribute traffic across multiple sensors, preventing single points of failure.
- Consider clustering or high-availability configurations to enhance the resilience of the Snort deployment.

Placing Snort Sensors

To achieve complete visibility and effective threat detection, it is essential to strategically place Snort sensors within the network. The extent and depth of analysis, which affect Snort's capacity to identify and react to security threats, are determined by the placement of sensors.

Perimeter Monitoring

Placing Snort sensors at the network perimeter is a common strategy for monitoring traffic entering and leaving the organization. This placement allows Snort to detect external threats, such as unauthorized access attempts, malware, or denial-of-service attacks, before they penetrate deeper into the network.

Following can be the key locations:

- Deploy sensors at the ingress and egress points of the network, such as internet gateways and firewall interfaces.
- Monitor traffic between the organization and external partners or cloud services to detect potential threats in third-party communications.

Internal Network Segments

Monitoring internal network segments is crucial for detecting lateral movement, insider threats, and unauthorized access within the organization. Snort sensors in internal segments can identify suspicious activities that bypass perimeter defenses or originate from compromised internal devices.

Following can be the key locations:

- Deploy sensors in critical network segments, such as data centers, server farms, and sensitive departments (e.g., finance or HR).
- Monitor traffic between VLANs or subnets to detect cross-segment attacks and lateral movement.

Demilitarized Zone (DMZ) Monitoring

The DMZ is a network segment that hosts public-facing services, such as web servers, email servers, and DNS servers. Monitoring the DMZ is essential for detecting attacks targeting these services, such as web application attacks, phishing attempts, or DNS spoofing.

Following can be the key locations:

- Deploy sensors in the DMZ to monitor traffic to and from public-facing services, identifying potential threats before they reach internal systems.
- Analyze traffic patterns and anomalies within the DMZ to detect compromised services or misconfigurations.

Remote Access Points

With the increasing prevalence of remote work and mobile devices, monitoring remote access points is critical for securing connections from external users. Snort sensors at remote access points can detect unauthorized access attempts, malware infections, or data leaks from remote devices.

Following can be the key locations:

- Deploy sensors at VPN concentrators or remote access gateways to monitor traffic from remote users and devices.
- Analyze traffic from wireless access points (WAPs) to detect unauthorized connections or rogue devices.

Cloud and Virtual Environments

As organizations increasingly adopt cloud and virtualized environments, monitoring these platforms is essential for ensuring comprehensive security coverage. Snort sensors can be deployed in virtualized or cloud-based configurations to analyze traffic within these environments.

Following can be the key locations:

- Deploy virtualized Snort sensors in cloud environments to monitor traffic between cloud services and internal systems.
- Use cloud-native monitoring solutions to integrate Snort with existing cloud security tools and platforms.

Sample Program: Deploying Snort in a Multi-Site Organization

We will consider an example of deploying Snort in a multi-site organization with several branch offices, a central data center, and remote workers.

Central Data Center

Deploy Snort sensors at the perimeter of the central data center to monitor traffic entering and leaving the facility. This placement allows for the detection of external threats and unauthorized access attempts targeting critical infrastructure.

The deployments will be:

- Place sensors at the internet gateway and firewall interfaces to monitor incoming and outgoing traffic.
- Monitor internal segments within the data center, such as server farms and storage networks, to detect lateral movement and insider threats.

Branch Offices

Deploy Snort sensors at the perimeter of each branch office to monitor local traffic and detect threats targeting branch-specific assets. This placement ensures consistent security coverage across all locations.

The deployments will be:

- Place sensors at the internet gateway and VPN concentrators to monitor remote access traffic.
- Monitor local network segments, such as office LANs and departmental subnets, to detect internal threats and unauthorized activities.

Remote Workers

Deploy Snort sensors at remote access points to monitor traffic from remote workers and devices. This placement ensures that connections from external users are secure and compliant with organizational policies.

The deployments will be:

- Monitor traffic at VPN concentrators and remote access gateways to detect unauthorized access attempts and data leaks.

- Use endpoint security solutions to complement Snort's monitoring capabilities, providing additional protection for remote devices.

Cloud Environments

Deploy Snort sensors in virtualized or cloud-based configurations to monitor traffic within cloud environments. This placement ensures comprehensive security coverage for cloud-native applications and services.

The deployments will be:

- Use virtualized Snort sensors to monitor traffic between cloud services and internal systems.
- Integrate Snort with cloud security tools to provide unified monitoring and threat detection across all platforms.

Network design, security goals, resource distribution, scalability, and resilience are all important factors to think about when creating a Snort deployment plan. Organizations can protect their assets and data effectively by installing Snort sensors in strategic network locations. This allows for comprehensive visibility and effective threat detection.

Performance Tuning and Optimization

As networks grow in scale and complexity, Snort must be capable of handling increased traffic loads without compromising security or performance. This section will run you through the process of scaling Snort for large networks and maintaining a balance between security and performance.

Scaling Snort for Large Networks

Scaling Snort to accommodate large networks involves optimizing its configuration, distributing workloads, and utilizing appropriate hardware resources. The goal is to ensure that Snort can process high volumes of traffic efficiently while maintaining accurate detection capabilities.

Optimize Snort Configuration

Optimizing Snort's configuration includes fine-tuning detection rules, adjusting resource allocations, and configuring preprocessors to handle traffic efficiently.

We can simply enable fast pattern matching for rules with long content strings to improve pattern-matching speed.

```
content:"malicious_pattern"; fast_pattern;
```

We may also arrange rules to process high-priority or frequently triggered rules first, minimizing resource consumption for low-impact rules. Other than this, we can adjust the preprocessor settings to balance performance and detection accuracy. For example, configure the HTTP Inspect preprocessor to inspect only relevant HTTP ports:

```
preprocessor http_inspect: global ports { 80 443 }
```

Moreover, one can utilize the Stream5 preprocessor to reassemble TCP streams, enabling accurate analysis of multi-packet sessions.

```
preprocessor stream5_tcp: policy windows, track_ports
both 80 443
```

Distribute Workloads Across Multiple Sensors

Distributing workloads across multiple Snort sensors helps manage high traffic volumes and prevents individual sensors from becoming bottlenecks. This approach involves deploying multiple Snort instances in a distributed architecture.

A good way to do this is to implement load balancing to distribute traffic evenly across multiple Snort sensors. Load balancers ensure that no single sensor is overwhelmed by traffic. Following is a quick example:

```
load_balancer {

    sensor1: 192.168.1.101

    sensor2: 192.168.1.102

    sensor3: 192.168.1.103

}
```

We may also assign sensors to different network segments, such as DMZ, internal LAN, and remote access points.

```
dmz_sensors {

    sensor1: 192.168.1.101

    sensor2: 192.168.1.102
```

```
}
lan_sensors {
    sensor3: 192.168.1.103
    sensor4: 192.168.1.104
}
remote_sensors {
    sensor5: 192.168.1.105
}
```

And there is one more option is to configure failover settings to switch traffic analysis to backup sensors during hardware or software failures.

```
redundancy {
    primary_sensor: 192.168.1.101
    backup_sensor: 192.168.1.102
}
```

Balancing Security and Performance

Balancing security and performance is crucial for deploying Snort in large networks. The goal is to ensure that Snort provides effective threat detection without compromising network performance or introducing significant latency.

Fine-Tune Detection Rules

Fine-tuning detection rules involves optimizing rule sets to balance detection accuracy with processing efficiency. This includes prioritizing critical rules, minimizing false positives, and adjusting rule parameters.

Following is an example of rule optimization, wherein we disable low-impact rules and focus on high-priority threats:

```
# Disable low-impact rules
```

```
disable_sid 1000001

disable_sid 1000002


# Enable high-priority rules

enable_sid 1000010

enable_sid 1000011
```

Optimize Resource Allocation

Optimize resource allocation to ensure that Snort operates efficiently within available hardware and network constraints. This includes adjusting memory, CPU, and network settings.

For example, we can configure Snort to use multiple threads:

```
config nthreads 4
```

We can adjust buffer sizes for packet capture:

```
config daq: pcap

config daq_var: buffer_size=4096
```

Monitor and Analyze Performance

Continuously monitor and analyze Snort's performance to identify potential bottlenecks and optimize configuration settings. Use performance metrics and analysis tools to assess Snort's efficiency and make data-driven adjustments.

You can use tools like htop or sar for real-time monitoring. Following is an example of resource monitoring:

```
htop
```

We can also review the Snort alert logs for false positives or missed detections:

```
tail -f /var/log/snort/alert
```

We can use **snortprofiler** to analyze Snort's performance:

```
snortprofiler -c /etc/snort/snort.lua -i eth0
```

We can implement automation wherein we can automate the rule optimization based on performance metrics as shown below:

```
#!/bin/bash

# Script to automate rule optimization



# Check CPU and memory usage

cpu_usage=$(mpstat | awk '/all/ {print $3}')

memory_usage=$(free -m | awk '/Mem/ {print $3}')



# Optimize rules based on usage

if (( $(echo "$cpu_usage > 80" | bc -l) )); then

    echo "High CPU usage detected. Disabling low-impact
rules."

    # Disable low-impact rules

    snort -c /etc/snort/snort.lua --disable_sid 1000001

fi



if (( $(echo "$memory_usage > 80" | bc -l) )); then

    echo "High memory usage detected. Reducing rule set
size."

    # Reduce rule set size
```

```
    snort -c /etc/snort/snort.lua --disable_sid 1000002
fi
```

Organizations can effectively deploy Snort and maintain robust network security by optimizing its configuration, distributing workloads, and balancing security and performance.

High Availability and Failover

High availability and failover mechanisms are the strategies that enhance Snort's reliability and resilience, enabling it to maintain intrusion detection capabilities even in the event of hardware failures, network disruptions, or other unforeseen issues. This section will run you through configuring Snort for high availability and implementing a failover mechanism to ensure seamless protection in your network infrastructure.

Deploy Redundant Snort Sensors

High availability (HA) involves deploying Snort in a way that ensures its services are consistently available, even during hardware failures or maintenance periods. This typically requires deploying multiple Snort instances that can take over traffic analysis tasks if one instance fails. The foundation of high availability in a Snort deployment is redundancy. Deploy multiple Snort sensors that can monitor the same network segments, providing backup and load-sharing capabilities.

Following are the steps to deploy redundant Snort sensors:

1. If you are monitoring a data center and several branch offices, deploy Snort sensors at each site to cover critical ingress and egress points. Install multiple Snort sensors at each critical location. These sensors should be configured to monitor the same traffic, providing redundancy in case one sensor fails.

   Following is a quick example of the configuration:

```
- Sensor 1: IP 192.168.1.101

- Sensor 2: IP 192.168.1.102
```

2. Use configuration management tools (e.g., Ansible, Puppet) to automate configuration synchronization across sensors.

```
ansible-playbook sync-snort-config.yml
```

3. Use load balancing to distribute traffic evenly across redundant sensors, preventing any

single sensor from becoming overwhelmed. Following is an example of the load balancer configuration:

```
load_balancer {
    sensor1: 192.168.1.101
    sensor2: 192.168.1.102
}
```

And the HAProxy to handle traffic distribution:

```
frontend snort_frontend
    bind *:80
    default_backend snort_backend


backend snort_backend
    balance roundrobin
    server sensor1 192.168.1.101:80 check
    server sensor2 192.168.1.102:80 check
```

Implementing Failover Mechanisms

Failover mechanisms ensure that if one Snort sensor fails, another sensor automatically takes over traffic monitoring, minimizing downtime and maintaining continuous security coverage.

Following are the steps to implement failover:

- Implement heartbeat monitoring to detect sensor failures and trigger failover actions. Heartbeat monitoring involves regularly checking the status of each sensor to ensure it is operational.
- Use a tool like Keepalived or Heartbeat to implement heartbeat monitoring. For example,

```
vrrp_instance VI_1 {
```

```
    state MASTER
    interface eth0
    virtual_router_id 51
    priority 100
    advert_int 1
    authentication {
        auth_type PASS
        auth_pass your_password
    }
    virtual_ipaddress {
        192.168.1.150
    }
    track_script {
        chk_snort
    }
}

vrrp_script chk_snort {
    script "/usr/local/bin/snort_check.sh"
    interval 2
    weight 2
```

```
}
```

- Create a script (**/usr/local/bin/snort_check.sh**) to check Snort's status:

```
#!/bin/bash

if pidof snort > /dev/null; then

    exit 0

else

    exit 1

fi
```

- Ensure the script is executable:

```
chmod +x /usr/local/bin/snort_check.sh
```

- Use virtual IP addresses (VIPs) to allow traffic to be redirected to available sensors automatically. VIPs enable seamless traffic redirection during failover events. For example,

```
VIP: 192.168.1.150
```

- Ensure that the VIP is reachable from the network, and configure routing to direct traffic through the VIP.

High availability and failover mechanisms are essential for ensuring continuous protection and minimizing downtime in a Snort deployment. By deploying redundant sensors, implementing failover mechanisms, and using virtual IPs and load balancing, organizations can achieve a resilient and reliable Snort deployment. Through careful planning and configuration, Snort can provide robust security coverage in diverse network environments, maintaining intrusion detection capabilities even during failures or disruptions.

Monitoring and Managing Snort Operations

Effectively monitoring and managing Snort operations involves real-time monitoring of Snort activities, utilizing management tools for configuration and analysis, and integrating with broader security operations. In this section, we will explore how to perform real-time monitoring and use

Snort's management tools to streamline operations in your network.

Snort Real-Time Monitoring

Real-time monitoring of Snort involves tracking its activities, analyzing alerts, and ensuring that it operates optimally to detect and respond to security threats. This requires setting up monitoring infrastructure and tools that provide visibility into Snort's performance and alerting capabilities.

Setup Snort Logging and Alerts

Snort generates logs and alerts to inform you about detected threats and system performance. Configuring logging and alerting is essential for real-time monitoring. Snort supports various output formats for alerts, such as Unified2, syslog, and JSON. Choose an appropriate format for your environment and configure Snort to use it. Following is the example of syslog configuration:

```
output alert_syslog: LOG_AUTH LOG_ALERT
```

Then, specify the syslog server in your system's syslog configuration file:

```
*.* @syslog-server-ip:514
```

Next, configure Snort to output alerts in JSON format:

```
output alert_json: /var/log/snort/alert.json
```

Use **`tail`** to monitor alert logs:

```
tail -f /var/log/snort/alert
```

Utilize Real-Time Monitoring Tools

Leverage real-time monitoring tools to gain insights into Snort's operations and detect anomalies in network traffic. For this, SnortSam is a tool that allows you to manage alerts and take automated actions based on predefined rules. It can block traffic or modify firewall rules in response to Snort alerts.

To install SnortSam:

```
wget https://snortsam.net/files/snortsam-latest.tar.gz

tar -xzvf snortsam-latest.tar.gz

cd snortsam
```

```
make

sudo make install
```

Then, to configure SnortSam, edit the SnortSam configuration file to specify the actions and rules for alert management:

```
block { 192.168.1.0/24 } 300
```

This configuration blocks traffic from the specified IP range for 300 seconds upon triggering an alert.

Next, download and install Prometheus:

```
wget
https://github.com/prometheus/prometheus/releases/downloa
d/v2.27.1/prometheus-2.27.1.linux-amd64.tar.gz

tar -xzvf prometheus-2.27.1.linux-amd64.tar.gz

cd prometheus-2.27.1.linux-amd64

./prometheus --config.file=prometheus.yml
```

Edit the Prometheus configuration file to scrape metrics from Snort:

```
scrape_configs:

  - job_name: 'snort'

    static_configs:

      - targets: ['localhost:9090']
```

Then, download and install Grafana:

```
wget https://dl.grafana.com/oss/release/grafana-
8.1.1.linux-amd64.tar.gz

tar -zxvf grafana-8.1.1.linux-amd64.tar.gz
```

```
cd grafana-8.1.1

./bin/grafana-server
```

Add Prometheus as a data source in Grafana and create dashboards to visualize Snort metrics and alerts.

Integrate with Security Information and Event Management (SIEM) Systems

Integrating Snort with a SIEM system enhances real-time monitoring by providing centralized log management, correlation, and analysis. For this, use a SIEM platform like Splunk or Elasticsearch to aggregate and analyze Snort logs and alerts.

Following is the example of Splunk integration:

```
splunk install app snort_technology_add-on_for_splunk.spl
```

Then, cnfigure Splunk to parse and analyze Snort logs:

```
[monitor:///var/log/snort/alert]

disabled = false

sourcetype = snort_alert
```

Create Splunk dashboards to visualize Snort alerts and correlate events with other data sources. After this, use Filebeat to send Snort logs to Elasticsearch for indexing and analysis:

```
filebeat.inputs:

  - type: log

    paths:

      - /var/log/snort/alert


output.elasticsearch:

  hosts: ["http://localhost:9200"]
```

Then, create Kibana dashboards to visualize Snort alerts and performance metrics.

Management Tools in Snort

Snort provides various management tools that simplify configuration, analysis, and maintenance. These tools help automate tasks, manage rule sets, and optimize Snort operations.

Snort Rules Management

PulledPork is a popular tool for managing Snort rule sets, automating updates, and maintaining configuration files. First, download and install PulledPork as shown below:

```
git clone https://github.com/shirkdog/pulledpork.git

cd pulledpork

chmod +x pulledpork.pl
```

Then, edit the PulledPork configuration file to specify the rule sources and directories:

```
rule_url=https://www.snort.org/rules/snortrules-
snapshot.tar.gz|<oinkcode>

rule_dir=/etc/snort/rules

local_rules=/etc/snort/rules/local.rules

sid_msg=/etc/snort/sid-msg.map
```

Run PulledPork to update Snort rules:

```
./pulledpork.pl -c pulledpork.conf -g
```

There is Snorby which is a web-based interface for managing Snort rules and alerts. It provides a user-friendly platform for analyzing and configuring Snort operations. You can download and install Snorby as shown below:

```
git clone https://github.com/Snorby/snorby.git

cd snorby

bundle install
```

```
rake snorby:setup
```

Edit the Snorby configuration file to connect to Snort's database and configure alert settings:

```
production:
  adapter: mysql2
  database: snort
  username: snorby_user
  password: your_password
  host: localhost
```

And then finally access the Snorby through a web browser to manage rules and alerts.

Snort Configuration Management

Configuration management tools simplify the process of deploying and maintaining Snort configurations across multiple sensors. You can use Ansible to automate the deployment and management of Snort configurations across a distributed network of sensors.

Now, to install Ansible on your management server:

```
sudo apt-get install ansible
```

Then, create a playbook to synchronize Snort configurations:

```
---
- name: Deploy Snort Configuration
  hosts: snort_sensors
  tasks:
    - name: Copy Snort configuration
      copy:
        src: /etc/snort/snort.conf
```

```
        dest: /etc/snort/snort.conf

    - name: Restart Snort

      service:

        name: snort

        state: restarted
```

Run the playbook to deploy configurations across Snort sensors:

```
ansible-playbook deploy-snort-config.yml
```

There is Puppet which is another configuration management tool that automates the deployment and maintenance of Snort configurations. You can install it on your management server:

```
sudo apt-get install puppet
```

Then, develop Puppet manifests to manage Snort configurations, ensuring consistency and compliance across all sensors.

Following is an example to create a manifest to configure Snort sensors:

```
node 'snort_sensor' {

  file { '/etc/snort/snort.conf':

    ensure  => file,

    source  => 'puppet:///modules/snort/snort.conf',

    require => Package['snort'],

  }


  service { 'snort':

    ensure  => running,
```

```
    enable  => true,
    require => File['/etc/snort/snort.conf'],
  }
}
```

And then, apply the manifest to manage Snort configurations:

```
puppet apply snort-config.pp
```

Through the utilization of tools such as SnortSam, Grafana, Prometheus, and SIEM systems, a company is able to improve its threat detection capabilities and gain insights into the performance of Snort. To guarantee efficient and consistent deployments across complicated network environments, configuration management tools such as Puppet, Snorby, Ansible, and PulledPork simplify Snort operations.

Summary

In conclusion, we gained knowledge about deploying Snort in a production setting, with an emphasis on the significance of thorough preparation, fine-tuning performance, high availability, and efficient management and monitoring. The first step was studying potential designs for all-encompassing Snort deployment plans, which would involve things like analyzing the network architecture, outlining security goals, and distributing resources to make sure Snort works well in different kinds of settings.

Next, we moved on to performance optimization and tuning, which brought attention to the fact that Snort's configuration needs to be fine-tuned in order for it to efficiently manage massive amounts of network traffic. In order to achieve a balance between security and performance, it was necessary to optimize rule sets, make use of multi-core processing, and distribute workloads across various sensors. Techniques for ensuring high availability and failover were taught, such as deploying redundant Snort sensors, implementing load balancing, and using virtual IP addresses to redirect traffic seamlessly during failures.

Finally, the chapter discussed monitoring and managing Snort operations. SnortSam, Grafana, and SIEM systems were used to monitor Snort in real-time and give insights into its performance and alerting capabilities. The chapter also covered management tools like PulledPork, Snorby, Ansible, and Puppet, which automate rule management, configuration synchronization, and deployment tasks. By utilizing these tools, organizations were able to simplify their Snort operations, guaranteeing that deployments in diverse network environments would be consistent and efficient. Overall, this chapter taught you how to effectively deploy, monitor, and manage

Snort in a production environment, resulting in robust and reliable intrusion detection capabilities.

Index

T

U

V

W

Epilogue

I hope that by the time you finish this Snort 3 QuickStart Pro, you will feel prepared to install and administer Snort with confidence in your network settings. Writing this book has been a rewarding experience, motivated by my passion for cybersecurity and a desire to share practical insights that can help you in your professional journey. Throughout this book, we've looked at Snort's capabilities, from configuring it to meet different needs to implementing custom rules to improve its detection abilities. You've learned how to scale Snort for large networks, so it can handle high traffic volumes efficiently. We've also covered how to integrate Snort with other security tools, resulting in a layered defense capable of adapting to the changing threat landscape.

One of the most important aspects we've discussed is the need for Snort to be monitored and managed continuously. By implementing the tools and strategies outlined in this book, you can ensure that Snort remains a critical component of your security infrastructure, providing you with the insights you need to respond to incidents quickly and efficiently. I encourage you to continue experimenting, exploring new configurations, and tailoring Snort to your organization's specific requirements. Whether you are an experienced security professional or new to the field, the knowledge you have gained here will serve as a foundation for future growth and exploration.

Thank you for participating in this learning experience with me. Your commitment to understanding and implementing Snort 3 demonstrates a commitment to securing digital environments in an age when cybersecurity is more important than ever. I hope that the insights and strategies presented in this book will be useful in your efforts to protect your network and stay ahead of potential threats. As we say our goodbyes, may all your cybersecurity activities be fruitful, and may you never stop looking for ways to expand your knowledge. Snort is a powerful tool, and with the right knowledge and approach, you can fully utilize it to protect your organization's assets and data.

Thank you again for selecting Snort 3 QuickStart Pro as your starting point.

Thank You

www.ingramcontent.com/pod-product-compliance
Lightning Source LLC
Chambersburg PA
CBHW080214170726
48282CB00030B/1114
9788197416538